Site Planning and Community Design for Great Neighborhoods

Frederick D. Jarvis
Principal, Director of Land Planning
LDR International, Inc.

Home Builder Press
National Association of Home Builders
1201 15th Street, NW
Washington, DC 20005-2800

Site Planning and Community Design for Great Neighborhoods
ISBN 0-86718-384-5

© 1993 by Home Builder Press® of the National Association of Home Builders of the United States of America

Most of the illustrations, cartoons, and photographs in this book appear courtesy of LDR International, Inc.; all photographs or illustrations from other sources are reproduced by permission, and include specific credit lines.

Printed in the United States of America.

Library of Congress Cataloging-in-Publication Data

Jarvis, Frederick D., 1944-
    Site planning and community design for great neighborhoods/
Frederick D. Jarvis.
        p.   cm.
    ISBN 0-86718-384-5
    1. Housing development--United States. 2. Land use--United
States--Planning.   I. Title.
HD259.J37   1993
307.1'216'0973--dc20   92-43328
                                                    CIP

For further information please contact –

Home Builder Press ®
National Association of Home Builders
1201 15th Street, NW
Washington, DC 20005-2800
(800) 223-2665

1/93 3,000 Bookcrafters
3/95 2,500 Bookcrafters
9/98 1,000 Graphic Communications

Contents

About the Author

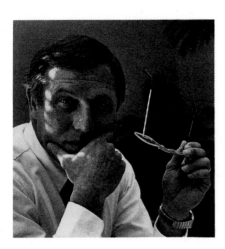

Frederick D. Jarvis is Director of Land Planning and one of the founding partners of the professional consulting firm of LDR International, Inc. of Columbia, Maryland and London, England. LDR provides planning, landscape architecture, urban design, and environmental science services throughout the United States and internationally.

Prior to joining LDR, Fred worked for the Rouse Company, the developers of the new town of Columbia, Maryland. His experience with the planning of Columbia and site planning within its villages and neighborhoods paved the way for his future work with builders and developers. At LDR, Fred has directed and managed much of the company's outstanding work in planning, designing, and implementing residential neighborhoods and communities. His accomplishments have ranged from planning new towns to small clusters and infill sites. One of his recent specialties has been the planning and design of golf, recreation, and waterfront communities.

Fred has written extensively on cost-effective site planning and is a frequent seminar speaker, panelist, and awards critic on the subject of quality residential development. He is the author of *Planning for Housing*, published by NAHB in 1980.

Acknowledgments

Thanks are in order to the many individuals who assisted in the research, discussions, and preparation of this publication. Particular thanks to the following: My partners and staff at LDR, for their consistent encouragement and support over the years; Diana Rich, for assistance in writing, organizing, and editing; Patrick Mullaly, for graphic design and layout; Eric Hyne, for special assistance with cartoons and graphic figures; Data Chromatics, Inc., for the production of plan templates and three-dimensional modeling of plans; Dan Levitan of the Greenman Group, who wrote the section on Market Evaluation in chapter 3; Joseph R. Molinaro, Project Manager for NAHB; and Carol E. Soble, Copy Editor.

This book would not have been possible without the guidance and support of NAHB's Land Developers Committee and the Land Development Services Department. In addition, the book was produced under the general direction of Kent Colton, NAHB Executive Vice President, in association with NAHB staff members James E. Johnson, Jr., Staff Vice President, Operations and Information Services; Adrienne Ash, Assistant Staff Vice President, Publishing Services; Rosanne O'Connor, Director of Publications; Sharon Lamberton, Assistant Director of Publications and Project Editor; and David Rhodes, Art Director.

Creating Livable Communities

In this chapter:

- Qualities of Desirable Places to Live
- The Suburban Growth Dilemma
- New Directions

Patterns of residential development during the 1990s and beyond will differ from the patterns of the recent past. The factors that spell change are numerous and complex and, now more than ever, demand creative solutions. Developers, builders, planners, engineers, architects, and government officials must respond to:

- increasing costs for all types of goods and services;
- constrained budgets for families and municipalities;
- limited natural resources, especially water and fuel;
- increasing levels of environmental regulation;
- more community scrutiny of and public input into development decisions;
- decreased availability of developable land;
- more traffic; and
- resistance to change.

As developers and builders, we need to reexamine today's basic issues related to residential neighborhoods and adopt a more balanced and responsive approach to community building. Our attitudes as well as our methods must change. We must offer future home buyers more than just a lot with a house on it. We must build comfortable, affordable homes in well-conceived neighborhoods that are integral parts of well-planned communities.

Qualities of Desirable Places to Live

A homeshopper survey can help reveal buyer preferences in a given market.

When shopping for a new home, home buyers first consider a community and its neighborhoods. They seek out neighborhoods that meet basic criteria related to convenience to work, shopping, and recreation; satisfactory schools and community facilities; overall quality-of-life expectations; and the individual household's position and aspirations in terms of age group, income level, social status, and interests. Only then do prospective home buyers consider the design features of individual homes as the basis for the final purchase decision.

Developers and builders can influence the perceived qualities of a neighborhood through effective site planning. One of the first questions that a developer, builder, or planner must ask is, "What kind of place do I want this community to be? What preferences am I seeking to satisfy? How can I achieve those objectives?"

Prospective home buyers look for certain basic qualities in a community, such as identity, convenience, and safety. While they often hold traditional values, they also seek innovation and uniqueness. People want variety, interest, and choice, even though they often desire harmony, unity, and sameness. People want privacy but also feel the need for neighborhood surveillance and security.

The qualities people seek for their homes and communities often appear to represent opposing points of view. With skillful planning, however, communities can achieve a balance that meets apparently conflicting desires. For example, attention to landscape detail can contribute to a feeling of luxury in a community of affordable houses. In other cases, a developer or builder may make a conscious choice to emphasize one quality at the expense of another by targeting a specific group of home buyers who value that quality.

Figure 1.1 summarizes the qualities of desirable places to live. Figure 1.2 explains how these qualities are created and indicates how a balance between conflicting desires can be addressed. The measure of success for any residential neighborhood is how well implemented community plans and site plans achieve these qualities.

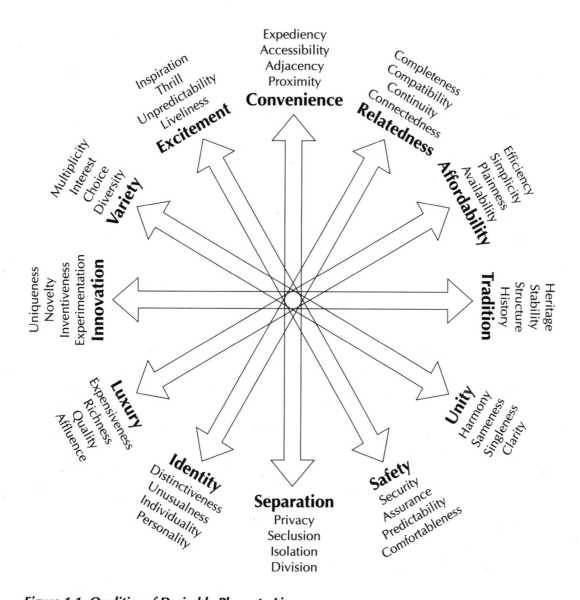

Figure 1.1 Qualities of Desirable Places to Live

Source: LDR International, Inc.

Quality	Definition	How It Is Created	Achieving Balance
Relatedness	Connected by reason of an established or discoverable relation, having a close harmonic connection, affiliated.	Community fabric, interconnected links, interdependence on other parts of the community, continuity of features, consistent themes.	A residential neighborhood is related to and a part of a larger community. While on one hand each neighborhood should have its own identity or distinction to set it apart from all others, it is also part of a larger whole.
Identity	The distinguishing character or personality of an individual, individuality, a mark of distinction.	Use points such as town squares or greens, orientation points, landmarks, natural features, or distinctive characteristics.	
Affordability	To be able to bear the cost of, to have the capability for providing.	Infrastructure layouts that are economical, efficient mixed-use, simplicity, basic shapes and forms, plainness that does not add unreasonable cost, compact.	As it relates to housing or a residential community, affordability is the ability to purchase the home and the things that go along with it at a reasonable cost. A determination must be made as to the level of quality and the richness of materials used throughout.
Luxury	Sumptuous living in great ease or comfort, rich surroundings, something desirable, but costly or hard to get, adding to pleasure, but not absolutely necessary.	Unusual or natural features, distinctive qualities, high level of site and architectural detailing, interest. Amenities, large size.	
Tradition	The handing down of information, beliefs and customs. An inherited pattern of thought, action, attitudes or institutions.	Preservation of natural, cultural, and historic resources, social values, maintaining architectural style, form, and characteristics.	Related to planning and design, tradition and innovation mean emulating that which has important value and disregarding that which does not. By some, the return to traditional small town planning with gridded streets would be termed innovative when it merely is a return to more traditional planning techniques.
Innovation	Introduction of something new, a new idea or method. Novelty, unusualness.	Incorporation of natural features in a new or unusual way, radical departure from the norm, contemporary or modern design.	

Figure 1.2   Achieving Balance

Source: LDR International, Inc.

Quality	Definition	How It Is Created	Achieving Balance
Unity	Continuity without deviation or change, oneness, singleness. An arrangement marked by even distribution of elements as in a design.	Organization, a hierarchy of parts, structure, clear and distinct circulation patterns. Oneness and sameness, consistent architectural theme and design details.	A certain amount of unity, continuity, and harmony should be present in any residential community design, but not at the expense of variety. A residential neighborhood should have diversity and offer choice and assortment. Dullness and lack of interest should be avoided.
Variety	The quality of being made of many different elements, forms, kinds, or individuals. Multifariousness, a collection of various things.	Mixed uses, varying size and combination of uses, spatial variation, hierarchy of spaces, undulation, landscape interest, seasonal variation, color, range of forms, heights, materials, ages, and period designs.	
Safety	Free from danger, attack, harm, hurt, or loss. The quality or state of being safe. Security and assurance.	Clear and distinct separation of transportation modes, speed reduction, appropriate scale, public safety and health care systems, "defensible" space, predictability.	In a community, safety not only relates to public safety, but also relates to predictability of real estate and property values. Excitement in a community might be created by social events or by an area of unusual design. The changeableness of one's environment has much to do with creating excitement.
Excitement	A strong emotional response, a thrill, intensity of feeling or reaction to arouse enthusiasm.	Unplanned evolution, lack of predictable organization, randomness, spatial variation, landscape interest, seasonal variation, surprise.	
Separation	A point, line, or means of division, an intervening space. The act or process of isolating, being apart, distinct.	Natural barriers, single use, singular functions, man-made barriers, cultural, social, ethnic, religious or racial differences.	A residential community might be divided into parts, sections, neighborhoods, or clusters which establish separation and privacy for individual homes. On the other hand, there is a certain need for closeness and convenience particularly as it relates to certain services.
Convenience	Anything that increases physical comfort, expedience, being in easy reach, nearby, or handy.	Adjacencies, linkages, goods and services within accessible distances. Clarity and directness, easy circulation patterns, mixed uses in close proximity.	

The Suburban Growth Dilemma

Until recently, new residential development was considered a welcome sign of economic health in cities and towns of all sizes. New homes meant new families, an expanded tax base, and a growing sense of well-being. Communities appreciated developers and home builders for their contributions to the life of cities and towns.

Over the last decade, however, public opinion has undergone a dramatic change, largely in response to communities' frustration over the negative aspects of growth. Developers and builders are now held accountable for traffic congestion, overcrowded schools, and inadequate public facilities. As "no-growth" fever sweeps the nation, the public increasingly perceives new development as a threat to communities' quality of life. The opinion shift has occurred for several reasons.

Lack of balanced growth. Most suburbs are bedroom communities that, by definition, experience an imbalance between housing and employment growth. As a result, the local tax base does not expand sufficiently to support the services required by residential development. Not surprisingly, bedroom communities are likely to favor growth in the employment base over housing development or to oppose any type of growth at all.

Lack of public investment. In recent years, government has delayed the maintenance of existing infrastructure and deferred investment in needed new facilities. Fearful of raising taxes, few local politicians have advocated costly investment in infrastructure. Instead, local governments have imposed impact fees and other assessments in an attempt to shift the costs of infrastructure to incoming residents.

NIMBY - Not In My Back Yard
NOPE - Not On Planet Earth
CAVE - Citizens Against Virtually
         Everything
BANANA - Build Absolutely Nothing
         Anywhere Near Anything
NIMTOO - Not In My Term Of Office

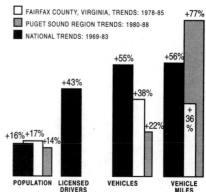

Figure 1.3　Mobility Trends
Source: Urban Land Institute,
Myths and Facts about Transportation Growth

Low-density, single-use zoning. Low-density zoning results in sprawling development patterns that require lengthy automobile commutes to employment and retail concentrations and thereby undermine efforts to conserve energy, reduce air pollution, and contain traffic congestion. Politicians and the public sidestep the zoning issue by blaming traffic congestion on high-density residential areas, commercial development, and developers. Low-density, single-use zoning has another important consequence in the many areas of the country where land costs are high. Requirements for relatively large lot sizes translate into high-cost housing.

Misconceptions about growth and traffic congestion. Many people believe that the increase in traffic in their communities is caused solely by new development. In fact, the nation's automobile dependence has grown at a much faster rate than its increase in population (see Figure 1.3). The average number of miles driven per year by each driver and the number of cars per household continue to climb. Thus, even with no new development, traffic would increase because of the population's growing mobility and dependence on the automobile.

Networks of no-growth advocates. No-growth advocates and environmentalists are organizing across the country. Growth is no longer just a local issue; regional and national interests are now involved in many local zoning issues and often effectively orchestrate sophisticated ballot propositions, initiatives, referenda, moratoria, and injunctions. These interests often dominate the local political discussion and pressure local politicians to embrace ill-advised antigrowth positions.

DO YOU KNOW THE DIFFERENCE BETWEEN A DEVELOPER AND A CONSERVATIONIST?

A DEVELOPER WANTS TO BUILD A COTTAGE IN THE WOODS.

A CONSERVATIONIST ALREADY HAS A COTTAGE IN THE WOODS.

While there are no easy solutions to the suburban growth dilemma, members of the home building industry, public sector officials charged with setting and implementing development policies, and planning and design professionals must work together to build consensus.

Sensible consumption of land. Future growth should be directed to areas with existing infrastructure capacity or to locations where infrastructure extensions can be made most logically and economically. By developing unused or underused land that is adequately served by infrastructure, communities can limit costly and land-consumptive expansion into areas lacking services.

Realistic funding of infrastructure. Investment in public infrastructure should be returned to a realistic level, with particular emphasis on funding the repair, replacement, and expansion of highway and transportation systems. Recent studies have confirmed the direct relationship between declining infrastructure investment and shrinking productivity and profitability. Investment must be directed to the maintenance of existing infrastructure as well as to new construction.

Mixed-use zoning. Planning for mixed uses in a community offers households the opportunity to locate closer to jobs, shopping, and services, thereby reducing the number and length of automobile trips. With more people in each household working and driving, however, it will be difficult to achieve net reductions in commuting distances. It is clear, though, that single-purpose zoning only encourages automobile dependence.

Effective strategies. No-growth policies and moratoria are not solutions. It is unrealistic for communities and their decision makers to believe that they can halt growth; instead, they should concentrate their energies on devising effective growth management strategies.

The development community, local officials, and the public should recognize their commonly held goals and develop more fruitful avenues of communication.

More Commuters Traveling Alone – Trend Bucks Environmental Imperative		
	1980	1990
Working-16 years and Older	95 million	115 million
Drove Alone	64%	73.2%
Used Car Pools	19.4%	13.4%
Used Public Transportation	6.3%	5.3%
Average Travel Time to Work	21.7 min.	22.4 min.

Source: 1990 U.S. Census

New Directions

The purpose of this book is to explore strategies for planning new development at all scales – from small sites that accommodate only a few houses to entire communities. As a basis for making sound decisions for future community growth, it is important to understand how current practices have evolved and what major problems must be resolved. In the next chapter, a review of the housing development trends of the past century reveals the successes and failures of various approaches that have been tried to date, including some innovative ideas that have yet to be thoroughly tested.

C H A P T E R 2

The Quest for Livability

In this chapter:

- Early Patterns
- Experimental Approaches: Garden Cities and Greenbelt Towns
- Suburbs: The Roots of Sprawl
- Early Cluster Development
- New Towns
- Planned Unit Developments
- Cluster Patterns Today
- A Quest for New Models
- Neotraditional Towns and Pedestrian Pockets
- Rural Villages and Hamlets
- Toward More Livable Communities

How did residential development in the United States evolve from the concentrated cities and small towns of the 19th century to the wide-ranging sprawl of the late 20th century? Where is the nation heading as the century draws to a close? This chapter explores the major trends in community development as well as some smaller but significant experiments and new directions. It also discusses the advantages and drawbacks of each approach.

This overview is not intended to be a comprehensive history of community planning in this century. Rather, it provides the perspective essential for developing community and site planning strategies and techniques that can lead to more livable neighborhoods for tomorrow.

Early Patterns

Traditionally, patterns of work largely dictated residential growth patterns. In rural areas, people lived where they worked – on farms. In cities and towns, people lived as close as possible to their place of employment; they walked or used limited public transportation or horse-drawn conveyances to travel to work. But the automobile changed all that.

With a fast, convenient means of transportation at their disposal, people could make new choices about where and how they lived. Changing patterns of residential development in the 20th century reflect the quest for more desirable places to live. City dwellers sought escape from crowded, dirty, noisy living conditions, while the children of farmers sought the economic opportunities and sophistication of urban centers. With each wave of prosperity and population growth, the home building industry has responded with new approaches for meeting the demand for more and better housing.

Expansion around the fringes of cities and towns in the early decades of the century tended to extend the established urban street grid. Larger homes on larger parcels of land lined the streets of the early suburbs. Homes located farther from the central core of the city or town tended to house the community's most prosperous families. These households enjoyed a variety of transportation options. By contrast, less affluent

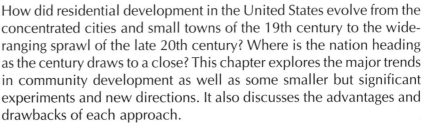

The Evolving American Dream   Reprinted by permission of Roger K. Lewis, FAIA

families were concentrated in center city neighborhoods and in housing near mills and factories, often within walking distance of the workplace. City streets had no room for green space; dirt and fumes filled the air.

Experimental Approaches: Garden Cities and Greenbelt Towns

Radburn, New Jersey

In the 1920s and 1930s, a group of visionary planners set out to improve the housing options for middle- and lower-income urban families. Inspired by the Garden City movement in Great Britain, a number of experimental neighborhoods were planned and a few were built. Among them were Radburn, New Jersey, designed by Clarence Stein and Henry Wright and begun in 1928, and the federal government-sponsored "greenbelt towns" of the mid-1930s – Greenbelt, Maryland; Greenhills, Ohio; and Greendale, Wisconsin. The greenbelt towns introduced superblocks of attached and closely grouped homes that faced inward onto linear parks (greenbelts) crossed by pedestrian pathways. Designed to reflect the balance among land uses and self-sufficiency that characterize small towns, greenbelt town centers provided stores, a school, recreation facilities, and offices. These working-class towns featured both greenbelts that ringed the towns and parks within the communities' boundaries. Unfortunately, without a mechanism to protect the greenbelts, development has, over time, all but claimed the towns' open space buffers.

Planners and government officials hailed the experimental towns as successful, but the communities' cluster principles did not find widespread applications. One reason is that little housing development occurred during the Depression and World War II. Yet, when the pent-up demand for housing exploded in the mid-1940s and early 1950s, a different pattern of residential development dotted the American landscape.

Suburbs: The Roots of Sprawl

The demand for homes created by renewed prosperity and booming population growth in the years after World War II led to the proliferation of the suburb. Land was inexpensive and public sector investment in an expanding network of highways made increasingly large areas of land around city centers easily accessible. As federally sponsored loan programs made homeownership possible for the moderate-income families of returning veterans, home builders responded by producing homes as quickly as possible. The "American Dream" became a popular term to describe the ideal living situation: a single-family home set on a lawn, far from noisy, dirty urban centers and factories.

Local jurisdictions without experience in development control attempted to regulate the overwhelming amount of postwar residential development by imposing rigid standards for roads and lot sizes and by enacting single-purpose zoning that prohibited uses other than housing in residential zones. Combined with the mass production techniques of home builders, local subdivision regulations gave rise to endless acres of nearly identical houses on nearly identical lots, all arranged in soldierlike order along wide streets laid out with blatant disregard for the land's natural characteristics.

Despite its many critics, the suburban development pattern that evolved during the 1940s and 1950s did permit the rapid construction of large numbers of homes. As long as land was plentiful and inexpensive and infrastructure costs remained low, the pattern was cost-effective. The maturation of landscaping, custom additions to homes, and the general softening that comes with age have improved the initial raw appearance of many of the early suburbs. With time, some of the older suburbs have experienced dramatic increases in value and prestige, while others have deteriorated, buffeted by such factors as poor locations and social trends that could not have been anticipated by the communities' original developers.

Even though it has its place in history, the suburban development pattern has many inherent problems. The seemingly endless extension of public infrastructure and services strains local budgets. The separation of land uses makes residents totally dependent on their automobiles, creating traffic congestion as the number of car trips continues its steady increase. In some areas, the supply of buildable land has been depleted. Regrettably, many of the ordinances that were drafted in haste to regulate the exploding suburbs have become accepted as immutable standards, and thus help to perpetuate the suburban development pattern.

Common Misconceptions About Large-Lot Zoning

• Low density is not the answer – increasing lot sizes only makes for bigger squares on the checkerboard.

• Large lots do not guarantee privacy.

• Low-density zoning will not slow growth.

• Large-lot zoning will not keep out "undesirables."

• Large-lot zoning usually is not the best environmental approach.

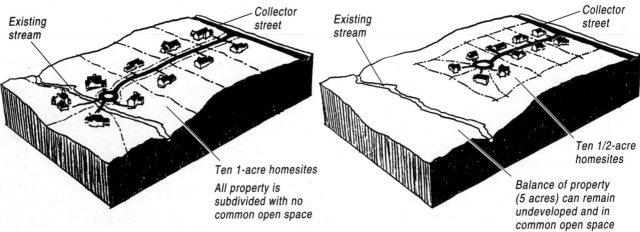

Existing stream

Collector street

Ten 1-acre homesites

All property is subdivided with no common open space

Existing stream

Collector street

Ten 1/2-acre homesites

Balance of property (5 acres) can remain undeveloped and in common open space

Figure 2.1 Clustering Saves Land for Common Open Space

Early Cluster Development

The early 1960s evidenced a reaction against the sterile, single-use "bedroom community." Developers, builders, and planners looked for ways to incorporate a mix of community features and values into their developments and to design communities that did not obliterate all of the land's natural features. The new solutions took the form of cluster development, which provides for a close grouping of homes on the most buildable portions of a site while, at the same time, preserving a large portion of the parcel (including environmentally sensitive areas) as undeveloped open space. The early demonstrations of clustering, including the greenbelt towns, featured attached homes or townhouses that enabled developers and builders to achieve highly compact development yet reserve the maximum amount of land for open space and community use.

The rationale for cluster development is grounded in environmental and economic concerns. When clustering is permitted, homes are designed on small homesites and on that portion of the land parcel that can be developed with the least disturbance (see Figure 2.1). At the same time, developers realize significant savings because shorter roads and utility extensions are required to serve the clustered homes. By scaling the roads appropriately, developers control or eliminate through traffic, creating a safe and comfortable environment for residential development.

The advantages of clustering can be achieved at any scale – from a few homes on several acres of land up to large-scale planned unit developments (PUDs) and new towns that occupy 10,000 acres or more. Almost 30 years ago, William H. Whyte predicted in his book *Cluster Development* that the cluster would become the dominant form of residential development. Even though cluster development is at the heart of the principles that guide the planning of new towns, PUDs, neotraditional towns, pedestrian pockets, and rural villages, the concept has been slow to achieve universal acceptance.

Resistance to the Cluster Concept

The cluster concept has met with resistance from developers, builders, and citizens for a variety of reasons.

- Many people believe that cluster development simply means increased density and multifamily housing. People also associate smaller lot sizes with lower quality homes.

- Communities fear that clustering is equated with uncontrolled growth.

- Poor examples of cluster development (inappropriately designed homes and site plans that ignore the land's natural features) have caused some communities to rescind cluster ordinances.

- Ordinances that impose higher standards on cluster development place an undue burden on developers; developers often find it easier to secure approvals for standard subdivisions.

- When development of cluster communities has coincided with economic recessions, the pace of sales and the financial returns have been disappointing.

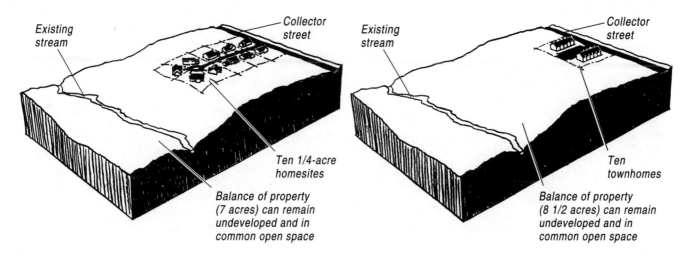

Existing stream · Collector street · Ten 1/4-acre homesites · Balance of property (7 acres) can remain undeveloped and in common open space

Existing stream · Collector street · Ten townhomes · Balance of property (8 1/2 acres) can remain undeveloped and in common open space

New Towns

With the reaction to the suburbs that characterized the early 1960s, community planners began to consider new, larger scale forms of development that addressed the monotony, excessive land consumption, and expensive infrastructure requirements of post-World War II residential development. The new town movement drew its inspiration from traditional small towns, the British garden city, and the greenbelt towns of the 1920s and 1930s. In contrast to homes-only suburbs, new towns integrated a broad mix of uses: employment, shopping, recreation facilities, schools, community buildings, and a full range of single- and multifamily housing.

The planners of Reston, Virginia, and Columbia, Maryland, pioneered the new town concept in the eastern United States, while, in California, developers of communities such as Irvine, Valencia, and Mission Viejo created new towns that responded to the West Coast lifestyle. In the 1970s, the U.S. Department of Housing and Urban Development supported further testing of new town plans with 13 federally assisted communities located throughout the United States.

A major feature of the new towns of the 1960s and 1970s was the clustering of homes and other uses on the buildable portions of the land, with the balance of the development tract reserved for open space. The open space was either left in its natural state or modified for passive or active recreational uses. Networks of pedestrian pathways

Columbia, Maryland

linked open spaces with the residential and mixed-use portions of the town. Thus, environmentally sensitive areas such as steep slopes, stream valleys, or wetlands remained undisturbed yet provided significant passive recreational resources for the entire community.

New towns typically were organized into several villages, each with its own village center that housed shops, small businesses, and community facilities (see Figure 2.2). Higher-density housing located close to the village centers placed many residences within easy walking distance of a variety of services. Radiating outward from the concentrated centers, single-family residences were clustered amid extensive networks of open space. The unifying focus of the new town was a town center whose retail and office uses served all of the town's villages but also drew patrons and workers from the surrounding region.

Aesthetically, the new towns differed markedly from both standard suburbs and older towns and small cities. The new towns were planned with a hierarchy of curving streets that channeled traffic from quiet cul-de-sacs to regional highways. The street pattern contrasted sharply with the uniform streets and platted lots of the standard suburb and with the grid pattern of older towns. The new towns' hierarchical road system meant that traffic volumes in residential neighborhoods remained low; tree-lined streets and cul-de-sacs created a pleasant, safe atmosphere. Yet, some people who drive the new town's curving streets have experienced difficulty in orienting themselves to their surroundings.

Grogans Mill Village, The Woodlands, Houston, Texas

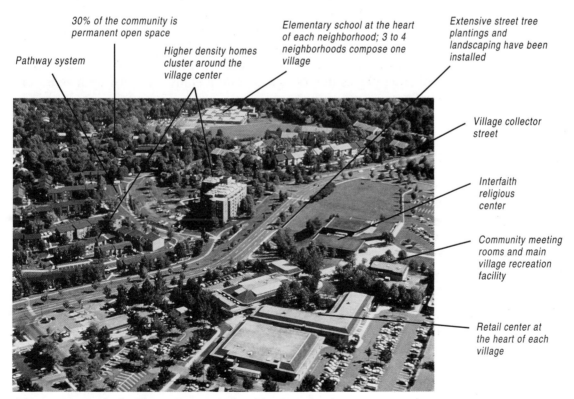

30% of the community is permanent open space

Pathway system

Higher density homes cluster around the village center

Elementary school at the heart of each neighborhood; 3 to 4 neighborhoods compose one village

Extensive street tree plantings and landscaping have been installed

Village collector street

Interfaith religious center

Community meeting rooms and main village recreation facility

Retail center at the heart of each village

Figure 2.2 Typical Village Center, Columbia, Maryland

Reston Town Center

Another major factor in the physical appearance of new towns was the use of strong design guidelines to control the aesthetics of everything from building exteriors to fences, signs, and landscaping. Many residents have recognized that the guidelines ensure a high-quality physical appearance, but others have found the results objectionably bland. And even though new towns deliberately varied housing types, the construction of large numbers of houses with repetitious materials and styles sometimes has resulted in monotonous streetscapes.

Many new towns suffered from financial problems that demanded deviations from their original plans. In economic terms, their large-scale, comprehensive nature and long-term buildout makes their development marginally feasible in today's market. However, some of the principles demonstrated by the successful new towns have been – and continue to be – implemented on a smaller scale in planned communities or PUDs.

The successful new towns have attained some measure of community identity and have achieved many of the social values intended by their planners. They offer a mix of housing types and income levels. A sense of community has evolved around shared school, religious, social, and political activities and interests. Some residents have realized the goal of a self-contained community where people live and work in the same place and thereby reduce regional commuting trips. In fact, recent studies have documented that as many as 50 percent of Reston's residents work in Reston and as many as 40 percent of Columbia's residents work in Columbia. Yet, the automobile remains the dominant mode of transportation, if only for brief errands; the extensive networks of pedestrian pathways are use mainly for recreation. And the town centers, often consisting of shopping malls, office parks, and parking lots, have generally proven unsatisfactory as public gathering places that offer a unique identity and provide a sense of vitality.

The new towns have succeeded in showing that cluster housing is marketable and that many families prefer a community with large amounts of open space reserved for common use, even though individual homesite sizes are necessarily reduced. In fact, the new town planning techniques that preserve the land's natural contours and vegetation have resulted in the modification of some site development ordinances. At the same time, the provision of community amenities and the advent of homeowners associations as a mechanism for ongoing maintenance and control of amenities have become widely accepted practices in the home building industry.

Planned Unit Developments

In the 1970s and 1980s, many local jurisdictions implemented special zoning ordinances to permit creative planning of neighborhoods in exchange for a variety of community and environmental benefits. A planned unit development is a legal mechanism in the form of a zoning bylaw that allows a more flexible approach to development. It allows the planning and approval of an overall site plan rather than the lot-by-lot approach taken by typical zoning. Planned unit developments (PUDs), planned residential developments (PRDs), or planned residential communities (PRCs) vary in size from 20 to several thousand acres. They typically combine different types of residences with recreation and community facilities. Some also include commercial uses.

The mix of uses and housing types in a PUD may be as narrow or broad as those typified by a new town, depending on the market, the aims of the developer, and the scale of the community. Regardless of size, most PUDs are planned around a unified image and follow comprehensive design guidelines that control architectural styles, materials, colors, landscaping, fences, signs, and other design elements (see Figure 2.3). Developers either offer a wide range of housing types or identify a particular market niche and design the PUD around a special theme or amenity. Golf course communities, equestrian communities, and marina communities attract specific home buyer markets.

As in the larger-scale new towns, planned unit developments respond to land forms and environmentally sensitive areas by clustering homes and other built facilities, leaving a large percent of the site in open space. PUD ordinances often allow streets that are narrower than those required by standard subdivision regulations.

Some PUDs have been criticized for a lack of diversity of housing product types and price ranges. For the most part, however, PUD ordinances have permitted innovative approaches to local housing markets, allowing creative developers and builders to introduce new product types and community amenities.

Examples of golf in planned unit developments (PUDs)

Minimal number of homes with direct driveway access to collector street

Street tree planting and landscaping

Pathway

Note different configurations for cluster streets

Cluster homes 6,000 square-foot homesites

Permanently dedicated open space

6,000 to 10,000 square-foot single-family homesites

Figure 2.3 Typical Planned Unit Development Neighborhood

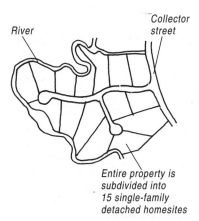

River

Collector street

Entire property is subdivided into 15 single-family detached homesites

Typical Sudivision Approach

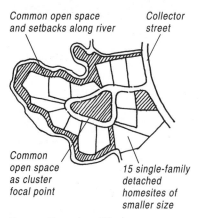

Common open space and setbacks along river

Collector street

Common open space as cluster focal point

15 single-family detached homesites of smaller size

Same Density Cluster

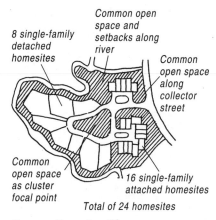

Common open space and setbacks along river

8 single-family detached homesites

Common open space along collector street

Common open space as cluster focal point

16 single-family attached homesites

Total of 24 homesites

Bonus Density Cluster

Figure 2.4
Three Development Patterns

Cluster Patterns Today

Despite the efforts of both the new town planners and the bold developers who experimented with PUDs and other forms of cluster development, many communities continue to prefer land-consuming, large-lot development. Admittedly, the cluster concept is not without problems in certain situations. For example, because cluster lot sizes sometimes are too small to accommodate standard septic systems, alternative solutions must be developed when public sewer service is not available. A homeowners association or similar authority must be established to preserve and maintain community open space and any amenities. Homes designed for standard lots may look out of place in some cluster layouts; therefore, site plans and architectural features should be designed specifically for the cluster plan.

The following points need to be emphasized concerning cluster development:

Environmentally sound. As stated previously, one of the main rationales for cluster development is that it is grounded in environmental concerns. Stringent environmental protection and subdivision regulations are now in place and more can be expected in the years ahead. The regulations cover stormwater management, sediment and erosion control, water quality, steep slope protection, floodplains, stream buffer setbacks, forest conservation requirements, and endangered species protection. In most cases, when a well-conceived cluster plan is compared with a conventional, large-lot subdivision plan of similar density, the cluster plan is environmentally superior.

Economically realistic. Another major premise for cluster development is that it often is a more economical pattern than larger lot, dispersed development. One of the major misunderstandings about cluster development concerns density. From a density standpoint, there are two basic types of cluster developments. The two types often are used interchangeably and thus become confused with each other (see Figure 2.4). With a same-density cluster, the same number of homes allowed under conventional zoning are grouped more tightly, using a smaller land area. With a bonus-density cluster, additional homes may be added to the base density to offset increased development costs or to achieve some special public benefit. Given today's increased cost of providing collective sewer and water services, additional density is often the only way to make a cluster proposal economically viable. Accordingly, it is important for both the developer and the local community to assess the costs and benefits of each cluster proposal carefully.

Collective sewer and water alternatives. One of the main challenges in accommodating cluster development is providing adequate sewage and water facilities. Because of poor soils in many parts of the country, minimum one- or two-acre homesites often are needed to accommodate septic fields. Health rules governing septic tanks have tended to steer development into low-density sprawl patterns that consume large amounts of land. Using cluster patterns, however, drain fields may be placed where the soils are the most suitable and away from water courses or drainage areas on the site. Many municipalities have discouraged use of community subsurface disposal systems or package treatment plants. Other municipalities have implemented a variety of alternatives to standard septic systems, however. These include individual on-lot septic tanks with combined disposal fields in an adjacent open field or common area; septic tank effluent pump (STEP) pressure sewers; grinder pumps; and water or wetland lagoon systems with spray irrigation. In the future, demand will grow for development of new techniques and alternatives to the costly extension of public sewer service.

Aerial view of cluster neighborhood

Tightly clustered single-family detached homes in Avenel, Potomac, Maryland

Total site area is 22.5 acres

2 units per acre or 44 homes permitted

Only 8.3 acres or 37% of the site is disturbed, which reduces site development and infrastructure costs

Existing wetlands preserved

Ideal orientation of homes on south-facing slopes

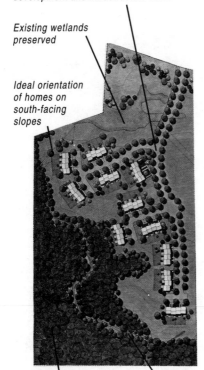

Less site disturbance and greater environmental protection. 63% of site in permanent open space.

Existing stream and wetlands

Figure 2.5
Typical Cluster Development Plan

No compromise in quality. A major and persistent public misconception equates cluster development to multifamily housing and assumes that reduced lot-sizes result in lower quality homes. This is not the case. Many people today prefer a lifestyle facilitated by maintenance-free homes and smaller yards. Many people are happy to own less land individually, provided they are guaranteed that the common open spaces around them will be preserved. With regard to the quality of the homes themselves, many excellent examples of cluster development have been built in all price ranges.

Permanency and maintenance of the open space. One of the biggest questions that inevitably arises in any discussion of clustering concerns assurances that open spaces will remain undeveloped. Most cluster ordinances typically prohibit further subdivision of the open space or residual property. Many jurisdictions even require that additional parties be assigned easements to preserve the land. Groups such as environmental land trusts, agricultural land preservation commissions, state-wide conservation commissions, or local conservancies can be co-signers and enforcers of such preservation easements. In most cases, maintenance of the open space is handled by a homeowners association to which each resident of the cluster community is contractually obligated.

More than just an option. To thrive, clustering should become public policy that is actively promoted as more than just another option. This concept is not new. In Massachusetts, for example, about one-third of the towns promote "permissive" (optional) clustering as an alternative for developers. A number of rural towns in Southern Maine and in upstate New York have had mandated (compulsory) clustering for many years.

Appropriate in a rural setting. When properly designed in context with its setting, a cluster development offers tremendous advantages over conventional, large-lot development (see Figures 2.5, 2.6, and 2.7). These advantages include: (1) greater environmental sensitivity and responsiveness to environmental regulations; (2) protection of neighborhood character by providing permanent open space for common use; (3) enhancement of the environmental setting and potential dedication of historic or culturally significant features; (4) creation of a wider variety of active and passive recreational uses; (5) creation of a more diverse and architecturally interesting neighborhood; (6) creation of a friendlier pedestrian environment, including walking and biking alternatives; and (6) reduction in the need for and number of automobile trips.

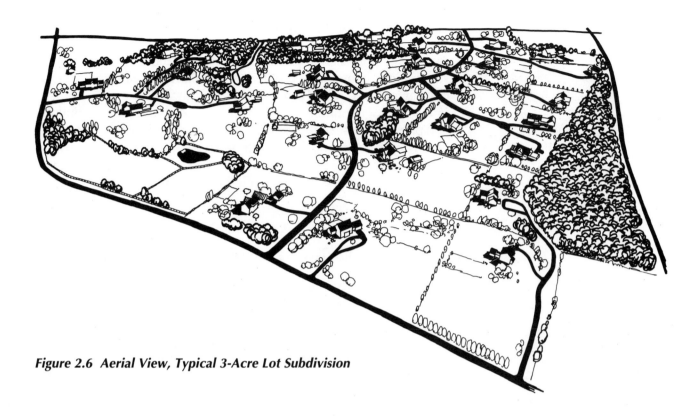

Figure 2.6 Aerial View, Typical 3-Acre Lot Subdivision

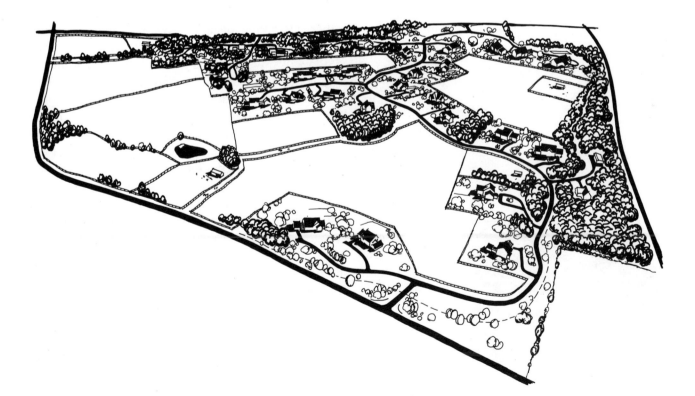

Figure 2.7 Aerial View, 40,000 Square-Foot Cluster Homesite Option, Howard County, Maryland
Printed by permission of the Scheidt family

A Quest for New Models

As communities debate their future growth and direction, standard subdivisions continue to proliferate. Standard and larger size lots are consuming land around urbanized areas at an alarming pace. Yet, even in the face of continuing resistance, innovative developers, builders, and planners persevere in seeking to create more livable communities that are both economically feasible and responsive to growing environmental concerns. Neotraditional towns, pedestrian pockets, and rural villages are examples of new models that are being tested in the early 1990s.

Neotraditional Towns and Pedestrian Pockets

Some planners have analyzed the characteristics of preautomobile 19th-century towns and early 20th-century suburbs in an effort to understand what makes a community livable. The compact, neighborhood-focused development patterns of these older areas are viewed as an antidote to the sprawling anonymity of the standard suburb.

Neotraditional development borrows many elements from these older areas, with a focus on creating walkable neighborhoods with a mix of uses that encourage social interaction. The ideal neotraditional town plan contains a full mix of uses – homes of varying sizes and types, shops, offices, schools, recreation facilities – all within walking distance of one another. "Walking distance" usually means an area coverable within a 10-minute walk or with a radius of no more than one-quarter-mile. Sidewalks, well-defined public spaces, and attractive buildings that flank the streets are intended to encourage residents to walk rather than drive to their various destinations. Every effort is made to de-emphasize the automobile both visually and functionally; residential garages and commercial parking facilities are placed at the rear of primary buildings, and streets are kept as narrow as possible.

A particularly distinctive feature of the neotraditional town plan is the street system. Neotraditional planners reject the curving, hierarchical street networks of the standard suburb, favoring a more urban grid, with homes set close to the street's edge. Service alleys provide parking areas, access to garages, and space for such necessities as trash cans and mailboxes. Neighborhood streets and the buildings that closely line them create intimate, identifiable spaces.

Kentlands, a 351-acre development in Gaithersburg, Maryland, designed by Andres Duany and Elizabeth Plater-Zyberk, is one of the first neotraditional communities to move into construction (see Figure 2.8). At Kentlands, which is planned for 1,600 housing units as well as for office and retail uses, strong architectural and site design guidelines ensure the consistent application of the aesthetics of older towns. Houses feature traditional materials such as brick, stone, and wood.

The Kentlands, Gaithersburg, Maryland

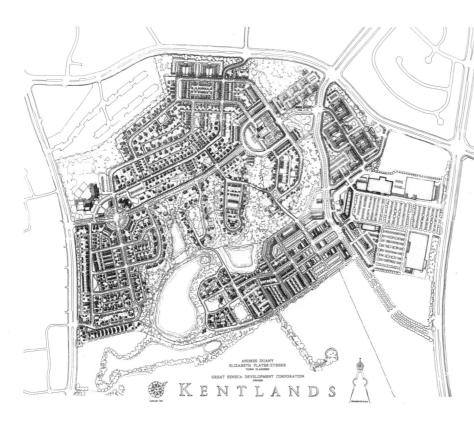

Figure 2.8
Plan for The Kentlands,
Gaithersburg, Maryland

Printed by permission of Andres Duany
and Elizabeth Plater-Zyberk, Architects;
and Joseph Alfandre & Company, Inc.

The Kentlands, Gaithersburg, Maryland

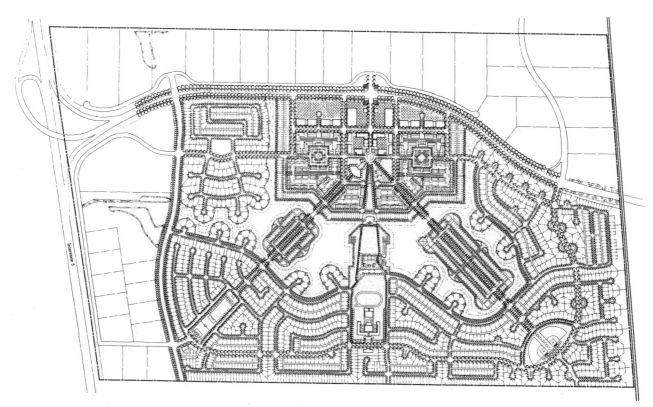

Figure 2.9 Plan for Laguna West, Sacramento, California   Printed by permission of Peter Calthorpe

A traditional neighborhood in Kingsmill, James City County, Virginia

Design elements such as picket fences visually unify the community. The gradual emergence of Kentlands will provide an opportunity to test neotraditional planning concepts, particularly the notion that internal automobile trips can be reduced. If Kentlands is typical of future neotraditional towns, however, external automobile use will not significantly decline. Virtually all Kentlands residents can be expected to work in other parts of the Washington, DC, metropolitan area. Once they leave the neotraditional community, they will face the same commuting problems as their counterparts in standard suburban communities.

Pedestrian pockets, by contrast, focus on reducing areawide automobile dependence by locating all residents within walking distance of a transit node. The pockets are intended to be located at one-mile intervals along a transit line, forming a framework for regional growth. While pedestrian pockets share many common design themes with the neotraditional town (a compact development pattern, a simple grid street system, narrow building setbacks, mixed uses, and strong pedestrian orientation), they are much less reliant on historical references in determining architectural guidelines. The primary emphasis is on encouraging transit-oriented development at a livable density and providing a full range of pedestrian-accessible community elements such as schools, shopping, daycare, and recreation areas. The first pedestrian pocket development is the 1,045-acre Laguna West, located near Sacramento, California (see Figure 2.9). Planned by Peter Calthorpe, this community will feature over 3,000 homes as well as office, retail, and industrial development.

Based on preliminary evaluations and initial market acceptance of these new models, certain principles are already evident. Successful pedestrian pockets and neotraditional towns generally will possess the following characteristics:

- one or more destinations to which people can walk, such as a transit node or a shopping center;
- high quality (ease and pleasantness) of planned walking areas;
- proximity within 20 to 30 miles of a major city;
- location in the path of population growth;
- on-site amenities and excellent schools;
- up-front investment in infrastructure and landscaping to create mature street scenes;
- a balance of curving streets, straight streets, and cul-de-sacs, and a mix of designs including homes set close to the street and homes with deeper setbacks;
- affordably priced homes, achieved through lot segmentation and an appropriate housing mix based on market trends and sound market research; and
- favorable economic factors and good project management so that the development is not burdened with insupportable amenities, punitive taxes, or special assessment fees.

Summary of Rural Village and Rural Hamlet Zoning District Ordinance, Loudoun County, Virginia

Village	*Hamlet*
Size	
100 - 300 residential units with associated commercial, office and civic uses.	5 - 25 hamlet lots; minimum 1/3 acre size; no more than 1 dwelling unit per 300 acres of open space.
Form	
Compact, 60 - 160 acres, village proper will be surrounded by open space known as village "conservancy," of at least 4 times the area of the village proper.	To be surrounded by conservancy lots and common open space. Minimum 80% of tract in common open space.
Physical Character	
Generally rectilinear pattern of interconnecting streets. Hierarchy of parks and squares, designated to preserve and enhance views. Must have central civic space or village green.	May be designed along a road or around a green square.
Location and Formation	
To be located in accordance with areas defined on general plan. Not closer than 1 mile from the edge of another village proper.	No closer than 800 feet to existing settlements.
Special Provisions	
Density transfer options. Density bonus for affordable apartments. Wastewater and water service to be collective systems operated by county sanitation authority.	Each dwelling will have a wastewater disposal system. Drainfields may be located in common space.

Rural Villages and Hamlets

The neotraditional town planning movement has led to exploration of the rural village and hamlet as alternatives for development in rural or agricultural areas. A rural village may be the planned extension of an existing community or a new settlement built on previously undeveloped land. In either case, rural villages involve more concentrated residential development than is typically allowed in rural zoning classes.

Designed as a substitute for scattered large-lot development, rural villages minimize disruption of the rural landscape and are intended to help preserve agricultural land. In some locations, nonprofit preservation groups have worked cooperatively with the planners of rural villages, using techniques such as land trusts to further ensure that the land surrounding the villages remains undeveloped.

The rural village is intended to serve as a physical, social and economic focal point in the rural landscape, building on and reinforcing the traditional settlement pattern. Although rural villages are seen mainly as residential settlements, they are also appropriate locations for schools, government offices, churches and stores. Small villages may be no more than a few homes located at a crossroads, perhaps grouped around a single commercial building such as a general store. Larger rural villages may contain a small "downtown" surrounded by homes. Hamlets are essentially smaller versions of rural villages.

Toward More Livable Communities

As the 20th century draws to a close, the home building industry can point with satisfaction to the nation's progress in increasing the supply of comfortable homes in livable environments. The variety of available housing types, the range of prices, and the multiplicity of living environments in today's United States are probably unmatched by any other country at any other time in history.

Yet, major issues affecting the quality of life in the nation's communities remain unresolved. Environmental concerns, increasing traffic congestion, and escalating housing costs are among the challenges to the home building industry and the planning profession in the years ahead. At the same time, home buyers will continue to seek – and expect to find – the qualities defined in chapter 1 that make a community livable. Figure 2.10 summarizes various features, assets, and limitations found in different forms of communities. The following chapters present sound principles of site design and community planning that can be used to realistically improve the overall quality of residential development.

	Feature	Assets	Limitations
Greenbelt Towns	Attached homes organized around linear parks with pedestrian pathways. Town centers with stores, school, recreational facilities and offices. External greenbelts provide buffer from surrounding development.	• Relatively high densities of housing achieved in green setting • Pedestrian orientation • Strong sense of community	• Monotonous linear arrangement of housing clusters • No protection of external greenbelts from future development
Post World War II Suburbs	Moderately-priced detached homes constructed in large tracts near existing urban areas, made accessible by highway construction and automobile ownership.	• Rapid satisfaction of huge demand for housing • Costs minimized through standardization and mass production techniques, and use of cheap land	• Excessively land-consumptive • Visual monotony • Little or no open space; natural features of land obliterated • Auto orientation
Cluster Development	Tighter grouping of homes on most buildable portions of site, leaving balance in open space. Cluster concept can be applied to both attached and detached homes.	• Natural features of land can be preserved • Shorter roadways and utility extensions • Shared open space available for recreational use	• Can be difficult to implement under existing ordinances • Generally requires public sewer service • Requires site planning and architecture specifically designed for clustering
New Towns	Large-scale planned community with all uses–homes, retail, business, recreation, community services – developed "from scratch" on raw land. Based on clustering principles, with large percentage of land left in natural state as open space. Design guidelines control visual appearance of buildings, signs, landscaping, fences, etc. Homeowners associations for enforcement of guidelines, maintenance of open spaces and operation of community facilities.	• Land use responding to natural features; extensive open space • Mixture of housing types and densities • Hierachical road system channels traffic from local streets to major arterials • Curvilinear roads respond to topography • Village centers and town center provide sense of community, convenient shopping/ services • Pedestrian pathway system, extensive recreational and community facilities	• Bland visual image; orientation (way-finding) difficult • Higher proportion of single-family homes than intended by original planners; few "affordable" homes • Pathway used primarily for recreation; residents highly auto-dependent • Majority of residents work outside new town and workers commute in, increasing regional traffic
PUDs	Concepts of new towns applied on smaller scale, ranging from a few acres to several thousand. Range from residential-only to broad mix of uses similar to new town.	• PUD ordinances permit innovative planning concepts not allowed under standard regulations • Clustering permits sensitive response to natural features of site • High proportion of open space • In large PUDs, assets similar to those in new town	• Many PUDs have narrow range of housing types and prices • Larger PUDs experience same drawbacks described for new towns • PUD ordinances sometimes impose higher standards, making PUD development costly
Neotraditional Towns	A variety of housing types combined with commercial and community uses are concentrated in a compact, walkable plan. Neotraditional towns are modeled visually and functionally on pre-20th century American towns, with gridded street systems and narrow setbacks.	• Appealing visual image assured with strong design guidelines • Street grid, landmark buildings, public spaces and view corridors simplify spatial orientation • Pedestrian orientation encourages reduction in internal automobile trips • Strong sense of community • Mix of housing types and other community uses • Alleys and rear-oriented garages reduce visual impact of cars	• Grid street/block pattern makes sensitivity to natural features of land difficult • Cost of implementing image elements of infrastructure (i.e., brick sidewalks) may lead to exclusively high-end housing or compromises in quality • Marketability of concept, feasibility of specific elements such as retail, and impact on regional traffic patterns remain to be tested
Pedestrian Pockets	Pedestrian pockets are similar to neotraditional towns in plan, but do not attempt to impose architectural styles or period image. Focus is on proximity to public transit to decrease automobile trips.	• Strong pedestrian orientation • Mix of uses to create fully functional residential community within walking distance of transit node • Realistic in assumption that residents will commute elsewhere to work	• Difficult to justify rail-based transit stop at proposed residential densities; first built models lack transit element or rely on buses • Functional requirements of rail transit stop (large-scale parking, bus and auto drop-off zones) difficult to integrate into heart of pedestrian-oriented community
Rural Villages	Similar to neotraditional town but adapted to rural setting. Can be extension of existing community or new settlement; size varies. More concentrated development than is typically allowed by rural zoning; pedestrian orientation. Often coupled with agricultural or scenic lands preservation efforts.	• Clustering reduces land consumption • Visual appeal and charm • Pedestrian orientation	• Provision of required public services can be difficult • Existing residents frequently oppose concept, fearing uncontrolled growth • Economic viability questionable due to small size

Figure 2.10 Community Development Patterns

Site Evaluation and Planning

In this chapter:

- Baseline Information
- Contextual Evaluation
- Systematic Summary of Findings
- Summary Site Analysis
- Market Evaluation
- Alternative Plans and Concepts
- Selecting the Preferred Development Concept
- Rezoning and Final Development Planning
- The Design Charette

Discipline

Verification

Justification

Communication

The design of any neighborhood or residential community begins with a study of the proposed development site and its natural processes. An understanding of natural systems and environmental relationships is fundamental to any prospective development project. Yet, time and time again, developers and design professionals disregard a site's natural characteristics. The result often is unnecessary damage to the natural environment. For example, throughout history, woodlands have been cleared and marshes zealously drained and filled to create new farmland or settlement areas. Today, even when developers and design professionals protect areas of obvious environmental sensitivity such as high-quality wetlands, they frequently fail to consider a site's more subtle environmental features.

Sensitive environmental design can best be achieved through a thoughtful and careful site evaluation process (see Figure 3.1). If developers and builders follow a process of systematic planning, careful market evaluation, and creative design, they will greatly enhance their chances for achieving environmentally sound and economically successful development solutions. Why is this process important?

- *Discipline.* The site evaluation and planning process imposes a level of discipline that requires careful consideration of various environmental factors that otherwise might be overlooked.

- *Verification.* The process permits delineation of critical environmental areas and factors for regulatory agencies.

- *Justification.* The process helps eliminate arbitrary design decisions, thus giving the final design solution greater validity.

- *Communication.* The process becomes an important part of the presentation package and is useful in selling and marketing the plan to decision makers and to the public during the rezoning or approval process.

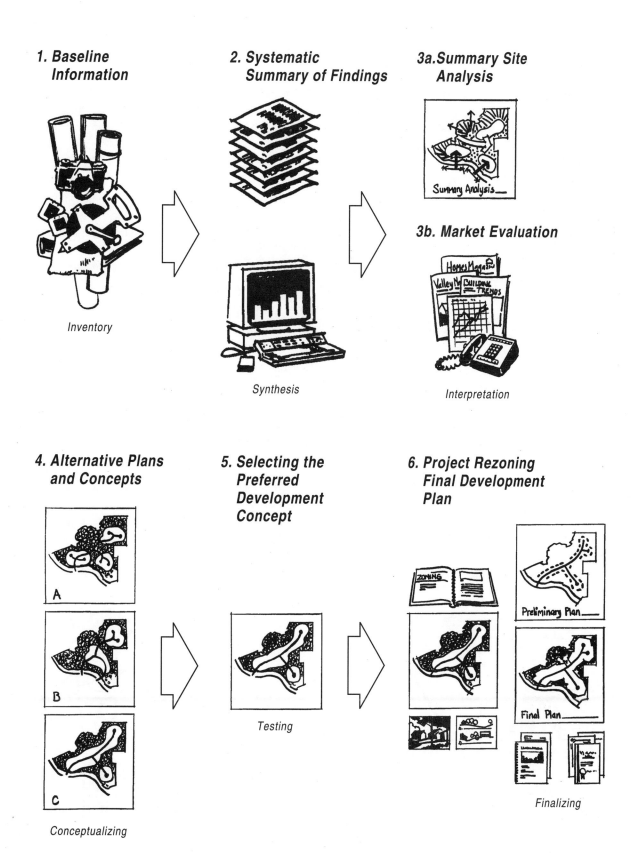

1. Baseline Information

Inventory

2. Systematic Summary of Findings

Synthesis

3a. Summary Site Analysis

Summary Analysis

3b. Market Evaluation

Interpretation

4. Alternative Plans and Concepts

A

B

C

Conceptualizing

5. Selecting the Preferred Development Concept

Testing

6. Project Rezoning Final Development Plan

Preliminary Plan

Final Plan

Finalizing

Figure 3.1 Steps in the Site Evaluation and Planning Process

Baseline Information

The first step calls for collecting baseline data, conducting a literature review, and performing an environmental audit or environmental site assessment (ESA). The following list indicates the type of information normally required in an ESA:

Natural Resources

- Land –   Geology, soils, landforms, ridgelines, slopes, scenic values
- Water –   Surface and groundwater, drainage conditions, tidal and nontidal wetlands delineation
- Vegetation –   Vegetative types and conditions, tree stand delineation
- Wildlife –   Habitats and endangered species
- Climate –   Macro- and microconditions, air quality, noise considerations

Manmade Features

- Buildings –   Existing structures, outbuildings, foundations
- Transportation –   Road network, transit systems, bicycle trails
- Infrastructure –   Sewage, water supply, schools, other utilities, or easements

Cultural Factors

- Social Influence –   Neighboring uses, historic and archeological values, community attitudes
- Political and Legal Constraints –   Jurisdictional issues, master plan requirements, zoning and subdivision regulations, location of easements, environmental regulations
- Economic –   Land values, taxation structure, growth potential, off-site improvements

Figure 3.2 Regional Context, Location Map

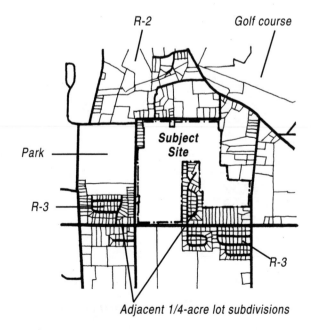

Figure 3.3 Community Context, Surrounding Neighborhood

Contextual Evaluation

Developers and builders should evaluate a site on at least three contextual levels: the regional context, the community context, and the site context (see Figures 3.2, 3.3 and 3.4). Regional context involves growth management policies; the condition and capacity of regional infrastructure such as roads, transit, and open space; the balance between housing and employment locations; and the natural and cultural resources that are peculiar to the region. In a nation blessed with almost every form of geographic subregion – mountains, plains, deserts, and coastal areas as well as cool, temperate, temperate-humid, hot-humid, and hot-arid zones – geography plays an important role in regional context.

Community context pertains to community infrastructure, public facilities and services, community development patterns, and local controls and regulations. Developers and builders must evaluate each site in the context of the local community's land use plan or master plan and development policies. Unfortunately, the provisions of a particular zoning ordinance or subdivision regulation may subvert opportunities for creativity. Developers who can clearly articulate how their new ideas will work within the regional, community, and site context have an advantage in trying to persuade local community leaders to accept or even welcome innovation.

Site context refers to the land and its natural features. A sound development plan should respond to a site's natural site features and be an extension of the site's environmental characteristics. Good design will appear to "grow from the land." It is also important to respect the boundary land uses of the site to ensure that a plan is sensitive to its surroundings, and to consider environmental issues that affect planning and development (see Figure 3.5).

Once the contextual evaluations of a site are understood it is much easier to arrive at a valid design concept. Ideally the design should be an outgrowth of the evaluations. But, if someone already has developed a preconceived design, the evaluations can be used to test, verify, or modify the concepts.

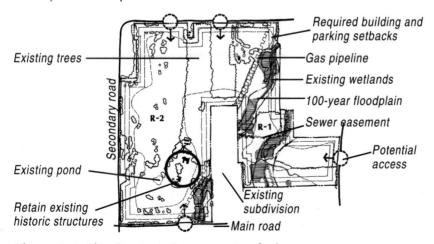

Figure 3.4 Site Context, Summary Analysis

Environmental Issues	Statutes	Requirements, Comments
1. Wetlands (tidal, nontidal)	Section 404 of the 1972 Clean Water Act; Executive Order 11190; state statutes	• Thorough environmental analysis • Locate in accordance with most up-to-date delineation procedures • Obtain second opinion • Determine quality of wetlands (function and value) • Propose alternative analysis • Avoid if possible or minimize impact • Prepare sound mitigation plans
2. Floodplains	1969 National Flood Insurance Act; Executive Order 11988	• Avoid development in 100-year floodplain, where possible • Elevate structures in floodplains to base flood elevation (100-year floodplain) • May not elevate with fill in coastal zone
3. Coastal Zone Management	Coastal Zone Management Act, 1972; state statutes	• Careful review of local requirements • Understand plant communities and ecosystem types • Sensitive utility and infrastructure design
4. Tree and Forest Conservation	Local ordinances, primarily	• Forest or tree stand delineation • Design must meet reforestation or tree replacement formula
5. Stormwater Management	1972 Clean Water Act; Soil Conservation Act	• Investigate local regulations and soil conditions • Minimal increase or no net increase of stormwater runoff from predevelopment state • Approved stormwater management plan • Use stormwater management facilities as amenities
6. Stormwater Discharge/Sediment and Erosion Control	1972 Clean Water Act National Pollutant Discharge Elimination System (NPDES)	• Basic NPDES permit requirements, including storm prevention plan with sediment and erosion control measures; best management practices (BMPs); no discharge of solid waste, including building materials; NPDES permits from EPA or from the state
7. Maximum Slope Standards, Grading	Local Ordinances	• Prepare slope suitability map • Investigate soil and geologic features • Try to maintain natural slopes and vegetation
8. Rare, Threatened, or Endangered Species	1973 Endangered Species Act; state statutes	• Determine if any species occur on the property • Identify critical habitats • Work closely with local government jurisdictions • Prepare Habitat Conservation Plan
9. Water Conservation	1985 Water Resources Planning Act; state statutes	• Sensitive land and water resource analysis • Land planning and site planning to conserve and manage water, cluster planning • Water-sensitive landscape design

Figure 3.5 Environmental Issues in Site Evaluation

Source LDR International Inc.

Environmental Issues	Statutes	Requirements, Comments
10. Air Quality	1970 Clean Air Act; 1990 Clean Air Act amendments	• Determine environmental impact • Conform with state regulations
11. Historic and Archaeological Significance	1966 National Historic Preservation Act; state statutes; local historic preservation acts	• Any project involving a federal permitting process requires compliance with Section 106 of the National Historic Preservation Act • Phase I Archaeological Assessment • Preserve historic site features and minimize impact
12. Hazardous Waste and Contamination	Super Fund Amendments and Reauthorization Act; Toxic Substances Control Act; Resource Conservation Recovery Act	• Phase I, II, or III assessments as required • Many of these studies are now required by banks and lending institutions • Cleanup of site may be required
13. Noise	1972 Noise Control Act	• Evaluate the site to determine various decibel levels • Separate residential homes from noise sources • Use earth berms and vegetation or structural barriers, if necessary
14. Critical Environmental Area Designation	Federal and state statutes	• Special environmental assessment or environmental impact statement • Adhere to local or regional requirements
15. Water Supply	Safe Drinking Water Act; state and local ordinances	• Drinking water standards for public wells
16. Groundwater	State and local ordinances	• Septic system standards, e.g., separation distance to wells, minimum lot size

Systematic Summary of Findings

Once collected, the basic information must be organized to permit an easy evaluation of the possible development options. The evaluation can be performed either manually, through the creation of exhibits or overlays, or by using computer applications. Computer technology for land development has advanced considerably over the last decade. Computer-aided design and drafting (CADD) tools are the most visible extension of this technology.

The newest technology permits rapid and inexpensive evaluation of such factors as market potential, environmental constraints, and engineering limitations. Inexpensive data purchased from such sources as the U.S. Bureau of the Census now are used for the rapid determination of demographic and socioeconomic trends when incorporated into a geographic information system (GIS). The use of a GIS permits the analysis of many complex, interrelated items such as environmental constraints, severe slopes, and stormwater runoff. Remotely sensed data captured from commercial satellites often help evaluate the feasibility of large-scale projects.

Computer technology also can be used to create a highly realistic representation of the appearance of a developed community. Whether modeled through the use of a three-dimensional CADD system or created with video simulation, the results provide a valuable communication tool for the review process.

Summary Site Analysis

One of the most important parts of any comprehensive site evaluation, a summary site analysis illustrates the interrelationship of a site's spatial, natural, and cultural conditions. The analysis should delineate the portion of the parcel most suited to development as well as any ecologically sensitive areas. Areas in need of more detailed evaluation also should be identified.

A complete and well-substantiated site analysis map is as indispensable to the land planning process as a navigational chart is to a pilot (see Figure 3.6). A few tips for preparing the summary site analysis follow:

- A site analysis should be prepared even for a small, uncomplicated site. The planning of a 5- or 10-acre parcel can benefit greatly from a thorough site analysis.

- The analysis should be straightforward and present information in its most basic and meaningful form.

- Site features or conditions that most directly affect the development of the land should be graphically highlighted and illustrated.

- Maps should include obvious factors such as rock outcroppings or wetlands as well as more subtle considerations such as the direction of a prevailing breeze or an unusual specimen tree.

- The site analysis should be used throughout the planning and design process as well as in selling and marketing the community.

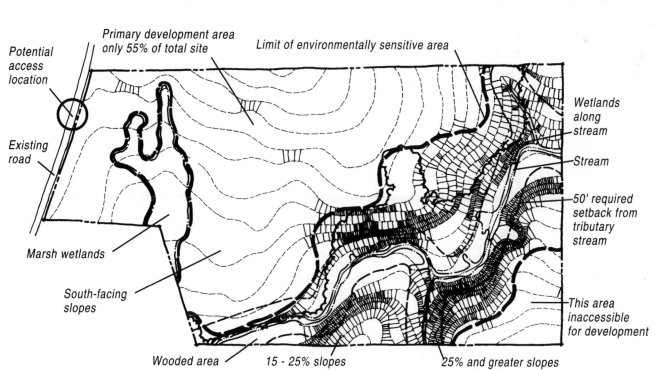

Figure 3.6   Typical Summary Site Analysis
Source: LDR International, Inc.

Market Evaluation

The market evaluation should be prepared concurrently with the site evaluation to determine a project's likely market demand and the site's realistic development and absorption potential. Formulating the optimal development scenario combines art with science.

Market evaluation demands that developers assume an impartial perspective. The market operates according to traditions and principles that cannot be ignored. Further, historically substantiated absorption rates and price points must be respected. In residential development, pioneering is best left to someone else.

A full market analysis investigates historical activity and current activity, projects probable future trends, and creates a development scenario based on fact. The investigation should extend to the following:

Economic factors. Current national, regional, and local economic conditions, including national trends, employment growth or loss, and local historical conditions are important elements in the market analysis. Developers and builders who are selling to area newcomers or to the resort or vacation market also must investigate economic conditions in the prospective purchasers' existing market. Mortgage interest rates affect prospective buyers' ability to purchase a home and influence consumer psychology.

Demographic and psychographic factors. Developers and builders must investigate household growth (or decline), household composition, family formation patterns, household age components, and income levels and lifestyle preferences on a metropolitan, county, and local basis and then forecast demographic trends for the life of the development (see Figure 3.7). Who are the potential buyers or renters? What are their needs? How does the local area differ from the overall metropolitan market?

Competitive factors. How many competitors does the market support? What are their strengths and weaknesses? What product is available? How well is it designed and marketed? What are historical sales and absorption rates? What is needed to create a unique selling position? The assessment of the competition must include an analysis of local and marketwide resale housing activity and an investigation of possible future competition in terms of available vacant land, homesite inventories, or projects in planning.

Site evaluation. Unlike the site analysis, the site evaluation examines area character, consumer traffic patterns, area services, and access routes from the consumer's point of view. What is the overall perception of site location? What is the prevailing housing type, age, and price? Is there a built-in market ready to be tapped? What problems, if

Figure 3.7 Typical Display of Median Family Income

any, will be encountered in generating traffic to the site? What will consumers see on their way to the site that may influence their perceptions?

Demand determination. The above factors must be synthesized into a realistic forecast of housing demand by product type, size, design, price, features, and so forth, and then translated into one or more specific consumer profiles. Who are the prospective buyers or renters? What are their needs, wants, and desires? How will demand be satisfied?

Site programming. Based on market demand and development goals, specific land planning design recommendations should take into consideration market positioning (entry, theme, amenities), neighborhood or village sizes (based on a two- to three-year absorption period), model and sales office locations, circulation patterns, relationships of villages to one another, waterscaping or sitescaping, and so forth.

Many traditional approaches to market evaluation can yield useless documentation. Check to be sure your market evaluation has been specifically tailored to local markets and has addressed the factors noted above. In preparing the market evaluation, the following tips can prove useful:

- The ultimate determinant of land value is the purchase by a consumer of an individual home (or the market rental rate a tenant will pay). Land value thus is a residual of home value in the marketplace. Because the ultimate consumer in fact determines the real land value and, therefore, project success and profitability, the developer must to the maximum extent possible satisfy the needs and desires of the marketplace.

- Many developers mistakenly believe that market research is valuable only during project conceptualization. Actually, market assessment must continue throughout the life of any land development project. This is especially important for long-term projects. Ongoing assessment enables developers to measure the effectiveness of the development's marketing, advertising, and sales activities and to make midcourse adjustments to residential product types, sizes, and pricing.

- Developers should provide the project land planners and architects with written programs before proceeding with the next steps in the planning process.

Sample Written Development Program	
	Homesites
Estate Single-Family 20,000 sf lots	40 - 50
Executive Single-Family 12,000 - 15,000 sf lots	130 - 140
Traditional Single-Family 10,000 sf lots	200 - 220
Patio Single-Family 7,500 sf lots	80 - 100
Single-Family Attached Cluster	80 - 100
Total	530 - 610

Amenity features to include: 18-hole golf course, river access, and boat launch.

Source: The Greenman Group

Alternative Plans and Concepts

At this point in the process, the land and site evaluations are merged with the preliminary market information to test the program and to evaluate alternative layout concepts (see Figures 3.8 and 3.9). It is essential to study several alternative land plan layouts. Alternative layouts can be generated inexpensively and rapidly with today's computer capabilities. Alternative solutions should be presented in diagrammatic form. They need not be carefully drawn or detailed in the initial trial process; it is enough at first to record only the essentials of a scheme. If the scheme bears up in comparison with other studies, it can then be developed further.

Insist that your land planner evaluate alternatives early in the process before you commit yourself to a final development plan. While some land planners may be content with their first plan proposal, seasoned professionals have learned that initial concepts seldom are the best.

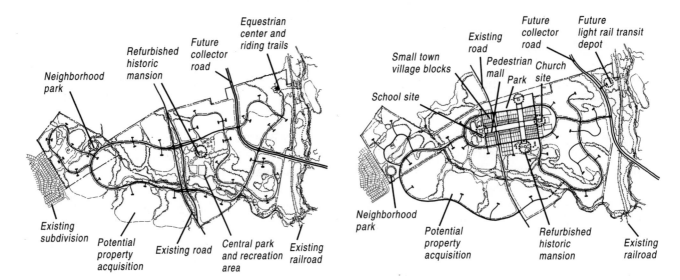

Figure 3.8 Park Central Concept   *Figure 3.9 Historic Village Concept*

Strategies for Developing Alternative Land Plans

- Do not be satisfied with the first solution.
- Do not assume that there is only one way to make a proposed project work.
- Ask questions that elicit multiple answers.
- Recognize that a lot of ideas create better solutions.
- Look for the second right answer.
- Ask "what if" questions.
- Challenge the rules.

Selecting the Preferred Development Concept

The preferred development concept (see Figure 3.10) will emerge as you carefully weigh and evaluate the alternative concepts. Your selection may be guided by the following questions:

- Which solution best satisfies the development's program requirements and best fits the site?

- Which solution best satisfies the quality-of-place objectives established for the proposed project?

- Which solution can be implemented? The preferred solution is not necessarily the easiest one to implement. In many cases, a rezoning or an amendment to local development regulations may be required.

- Which solution provides reasonable cost benefits? Conditions may not permit the realization of maximum benefits at the lowest total cost.

The preferred development concept is likely to reflect a combination of several ideas uncovered through the comparison of alternative plans. The opportunities and constraints related to the development criteria, the community's development standards, and local zoning and subdivision regulations should also be considered as you select the preferred development concept.

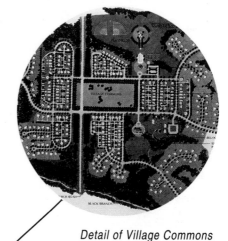

Detail of Village Commons

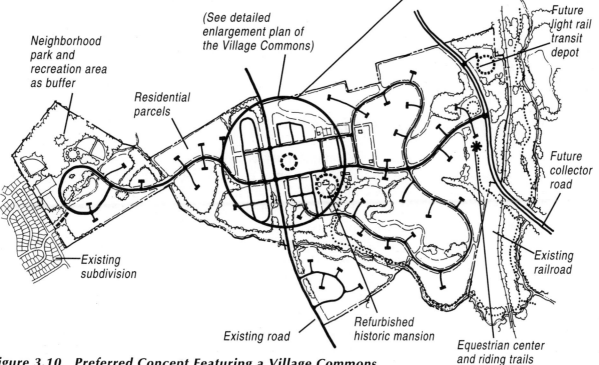

Figure 3.10 Preferred Concept Featuring a Village Commons

Rezoning and Final Development Planning

If the appropriate zoning is not in place, developers and builders will need to request a rezoning. It may be necessary, however, to demonstrate consistency with an approved comprehensive plan by amending the plan before the formal rezoning process can be initiated. The following tips will help in preparing to request a rezoning:

- Work with community groups and neighbors to develop consensus before initiating the formal rezoning process.

- Try presenting a conventional development plan or "by right" development plan to illustrate the advantages of your creative development concept.

- Use graphics and three-dimensional images such as perspective sketches, bird's-eye views, house elevations, cross-sectional views, or models to help others see your design concept.

- Look for ideas and successful examples in resource materials such as publications by NAHB, slide shows, videotapes, the Urban Land Institute's Project Reference File, and model ordinances; use them to show local planning and zoning officials innovative and creative approaches to land planning.

The planning and design process requires constant refinement and adjustment. Feedback and continued testing should be an integral part of every phase as the plans move closer to completion. With zoning in place, it is time to prepare schematic plans, preliminary development plans, phasing plans, final development plans, restrictive covenants, and development standards. When approvals and permits are obtained, the first phases of development can begin.

The Design Charette

A design technique that has recently received considerable publicity is the "design charette" process. A design charette is normally a two-day to week-long intensive and interactive approach to problem solving. The length of the charette usually depends on the complexity of the design problem.

The design charette is a coordinated approach that focuses participants' energy and creativity on solving site and land planning problems. The term "charette" is derived from the French word for "little cart." In previous centuries, French artists would hire someone to push a cart containing their paintings to the art auction so that they could apply the finishing touches to their work on their way to the auction. Over the years, the term has come to mean an intensive, often last-

---

Agenda for a Two-Day Design Charette

Day One

• Welcome and opening comments, statement of objectives	*Property owner/ developer*
• Overview of process and introduction participants	*Charette facilitator*
• Land assessment – with optional slide show or video of site, site tour; review of environmental and engineering issues	*Entire charette team*
• Assessment of regulatory controls, comprehensive plan review, zoning provisions, development standards	*Government representatives*
• Market assessment	*Market consultant*
• Working lunch – Review development issues, development goals and objectives, previous concept plans (if any), site program elements, staging issues	
• Several work sessions or one work session for core study group	*Core study group*
• Dinner	*All or core study group*
• Evening work session or presentations (optional)	*All or core study group*

Day Two

• Work session, presentation to client	*Core study group*
• Development of final summary plans and graphics presentation to entire charette team	*Core study group*
• Lunch	*Entire charette team*
• Final work session and afternoon presentation – findings and recommendations, other models, next steps, work assignments	*Entire charette team*

minute work effort by architectural and design professionals to improve their designs.

The charette process can be applied successfully to distressed properties, project work-out assignments, or infill development as well as to the design of new neighborhoods. This innovative and interactive approach to problem solving can save developers and community leaders much time, effort, and money through consensus building early in the project planning process. As an approach that should be considered for evaluating a site, the design charette can lead to plans that are supportable by and acceptable to all affected parties.

Charette Organizing Tips

To organize and hold an effective design charette, here are a few tips to consider:

• The charette facilitator should be an experienced professional who helps organize, program, and direct the charette process. The facilitator sometimes helps record information and is responsible for adhering to the agenda to build and achieve consensus. The facilitator may or may not be a design professional; ideally, he or she will have had previous experience managing a design charette.

• The core study group usually includes the design professionals, owner's representative, civil engineer, and so forth, who work as a smaller group and then report back to the entire charette team.

• If possible, the charette should be conducted on or close to the proposed development site to enable participants to make any necessary site visits. A comfortable, adequate workspace and an environment that fosters creativity are essential.

• All the necessary background data should be assembled in proper form before the charette. It is advisable to distribute a packet of background information to key participants before the session.

• Citizens may or may not be involved in the actual charette process. This is a decision to be made by the owner and depends on a variety of factors such as whether the development project is controversial and the extent to which openness and sharing are appropriate for the specific situation.

CHAPTER 4

Ingredients of a Successful Land Plan

In this chapter:

- Site Sensitivity
- Plan Organization and Structure
- Roadways
- Open Space
- Small Sections
- Trees and Landscaping
- Preserving Trees
- Streetscapes and Site Furniture
- Selling the Land Plan

How do developers or builders know that their proposed plan will be successful? What ingredients ensure a sound plan? By illustrating comparison plans throughout this chapter, we hope to highlight some of the principles that should guide the formulation of successful land plans.

Site Sensitivity

Example of homes fitted carefully into the natural landscape

Chapter 3 emphasized the importance of a systematic and careful planning process as a prerequisite to understanding a site and its natural characteristics. That process lays the foundation for evaluating the land so that the design responds to, respects, and enhances the site's natural features.

Land with great natural beauty and resources obviously requires extreme sensitivity in its planning and development to minimize environmental impact and degradation. Sensitive planning minimizes visual and environmental impact, allows the natural landscape to predominate, and ensures careful implementation and follow-through.

Minimize visual and environmental impact. Planners and developers must take great care to preserve, enhance, and protect the environment. The design must be carefully fitted to the site's natural features to accommodate development with a minimum amount of disruption. This approach is often called a "least change" design solution.

Allow the natural landscape to predominate. On sites of great natural beauty, the land plan should complement and enhance the site's natural beauty. To the casual observer standing on the finished site, the landscape should be more evident than the plan elements. This is generally true of the architecture as well. Indigenous and natural vegetation can be used to blend site improvements and buildings with the natural environment.

Ensure careful implementation and follow-through. Environmentally sensitive plans must be implemented with attention to every detail both during and after construction. Deed restrictions and protective covenants ensure proper management of sensitive areas or open space. Environmental reserves are often recommended for setting aside sensitive lands.

Of course, development of all sites requires some disturbance, and some sites can be improved with skilled manipulation. Site sensitivity calls for capitalizing on a site's natural characteristics and eliminating or improving on any negative factors.

Plan Organization and Structure

Even in nature there is organization and structure. Structure is also an important ingredient in a successful land plan. Structure establishes a logical framework that permits people to orient themselves to their physical surroundings. Structure in land planning refers to the way the plan is organized. In its most basic sense, it is the creation of the whole plan by the joining together of all its parts. Structure is central, and structure on a smaller scale both provides the foundation for and gives way to structure on a larger scale. Every part depends on the whole – and vice versa.

Two primary components of a land plan that determine a neighborhood's organization or structure are the *roadway system* (along with its resultant spaces) and the *open space network*. The two must be designed in tandem to create a cohesive whole and an organized, structured community (see Figures 4.1 and 4.2).

How Structure Improves a Residential Neighborhood

- *Substructure* helps organize a cluster or group of homes.

- *Structure* provides the framework for a neighborhood.

- *Superstructure* relates to the organization of a community, village, town, or city.

Source: LDR International, Inc.

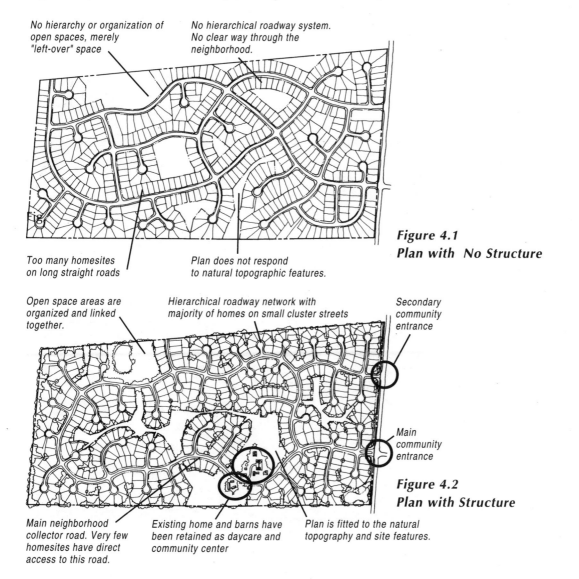

No hierarchy or organization of open spaces, merely "left-over" space

No hierarchical roadway system. No clear way through the neighborhood.

Too many homesites on long straight roads

Plan does not respond to natural topographic features.

Figure 4.1
Plan with No Structure

Open space areas are organized and linked together.

Hierarchical roadway network with majority of homes on small cluster streets

Secondary community entrance

Main community entrance

Main neighborhood collector road. Very few homesites have direct access to this road.

Existing home and barns have been retained as daycare and community center

Plan is fitted to the natural topography and site features.

Figure 4.2
Plan with Structure

Roadways

Since the advent of the automobile, streets have been the unifying force in the layout of subdivisions and residential communities. Too often, though, street design has been based solely on traffic engineering standards that promote high-speed automobile movement. Stated another way, street standards biased toward a "wider is better" philosophy result in streets that handle cars well but fail to accommodate pedestrians. At the same time, spaces created by wide roads and excessive setbacks tend to undermine the structure of the neighborhood.

In laying out a street system, it is important to keep in mind all circulation and movement systems. Developers must consider how the pedestrian will be accommodated – whether along the street, near the street, or entirely separated from the street. The placement of sidewalks and pathways and their relationship to automobile circulation are factors that significantly determine the structure of a neighborhood.

Problems with Over-Sized Streets

- *Over-sized streets encourage motorists to speed*
- *Overly wide streets are visually obtrusive*
- *Wide streets require more clearing and grading, and destroy natural landscape resources*
- *Land development costs are increased resulting in more expensive homes*
- *More paved areas increase run-off and add to storm drainage requirements*
- *Wide street pavements mean more maintenance and waste resources*

Overly wide streets can detract from a great neighborhood.

Pedestrian circulation should be considered as well as the automobile.

Street design should be based on and scaled to the various functions provided by streets. A classification or ranking of streets into various categories results in a hierarchical street system, which organizes traffic patterns to prevent congestion and other problems (see Figure 4.3). The following are some specific design principles that should guide the design of a proposed development's roadway system:

- Collector streets with curves and changes in alignment permit roads to be fitted to the existing topography.

- It is desirable to keep straight streets short for both functional and visual reasons. Short streets tend to slow down traffic in residential neighborhoods and minimize long rows of houses in straight lines.

- Narrower residential street widths and more sensible design standards, including reduced curb radii, help promote the development of pedestrian-friendly streets.

- Variations in setbacks and spatial dimension help provide open spaces to create form, activity, and recreation areas along roadways.

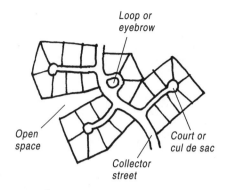

Curvilinear Pattern

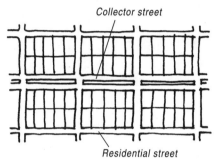

Urban Grid Pattern

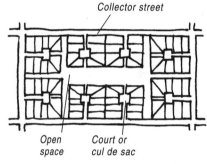

Urban Cluster Pattern

Figure 4.3
Examples of Hierarchical Street Layouts

A reasonably sized residential street

On short narrow streets sidewalks may not be necessary.

Natural open space areas are especially well suited for pedestrian enjoyment.

Open Space

Too often in the past, developers and builders overlooked open space and spatial relationships in the layout of residential neighborhoods. Yet, the voids and spaces between land uses and buildings are what provide form to settlement patterns. As the predominant spatial element in residential subdivisions, streets and building setbacks play a major role in defining a place.

Communities also need open space that is left unbuilt and available for recreational uses, preservation of natural features, or simply visual relief from the built environment. Providing space within and around residential neighborhoods is essential for creating an attractive and pleasing living environment. Well-designed open space becomes even more important as residential density increases or home size decreases. The following are some principles to help guide the planning and design of an open space network:

- Open space can bring visual order and structure. Neighborhoods should be planned to include a hierarchy of open spaces. Open space should be considered the circulation system for pedestrians, water, wildlife, and air. Open spaces are especially well suited for safe pedestrian and bicycle pathways.

- Open space can act as a visual and physical buffer in breaking up large communities into intimately scaled neighborhoods. Open space increases the sense of privacy by diminishing the sense of crowding.

- Open space can preserve important or sensitive natural areas such as wetlands and marshes, steep and easily eroded slopes, or woods.

- Open space systems can protect floodplains and act as natural flood storage and groundwater recharge areas. Protecting recharge areas helps maintain the groundwater levels that existing trees and vegetation need for survival.

- Open space can also be used for many forms of recreation. An open space can be set aside as a public gathering space or a formal park. As density increases, careful design and detailing of open spaces becomes more important.

A stormwater management area may also serve as a playground for the neighborhood.

Small Sections

The most successful residential neighborhood plans are usually organized around small sections (see Figure 4.4). Often, excessively large development parcels are transformed into communities that lack interest. As a rule of thumb, developers and builders are advised to construct 25 to 75 homes per section, cluster, or minineighborhood. The benefits of the small sections include the following:

- A layout using small sections is adaptable to a mix of product types and price ranges and permits creation of more diverse and architecturally interesting neighborhoods.

- Small sections in clustered groups are more conducive to mixed land uses, including employment centers, retail shopping areas, schools, and recreation facilities as well as housing; clustering also can provide more uses within a walkable distance.

- Small sections permit design flexibility that can enhance and facilitate a more comfortable, human-scale neighborhood.

- Small sections can be planned to be more environmentally sensitive and responsive to regulations that govern stormwater management, tree preservation, the creation of stream buffers, wetlands conservation, wildlife habitat protection, and water quality.

- Small sections create more opportunities to build homes with frontage and views to amenities.

- Neighborhoods developed in small sections can be more easily phased and constructed in smaller, cost-effective increments.

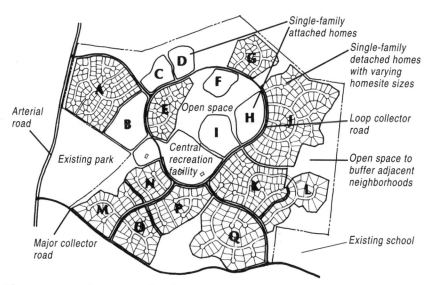

Figure 4.4   Plan Organized Around Small Sections

Trees and Landscaping

Probably no other site feature is more widely appreciated by home buyers than mature trees. Trees improve the quality of a residential neighborhood by:

- defining and organizing space;
- providing unity and scale;
- creating a sense of enclosure and privacy;
- providing shade and cooling;
- serving as windbreaks;
- softening the visual impact of undesirable elements;
- providing erosion control;
- adding seasonal interest; and
- creating benefits for wildlife.

Preserving existing trees wherever possible is the first step in planning the streetscape. Further, the planting of new trees should be considered a part of every new residential neighborhood. Plantings may be formal, informal, or a combination of both.

Formal planting incorporates an ordering of trees and landscape elements that provide a sense of importance and grandeur to a particular setting. Both native and ornamental plant materials may be used. The most effective formal treatments are those that are bold yet simple in design.

Informal planting incorporates trees and landscape elements as an extension of the natural landscape. Groves of native evergreens and deciduous trees can be planted to extend woodlands, while native grasses and shrubs can extend and relate to natural wetlands and marshes. In public areas and private yards, informal groupings of trees, shrubs, and ground covers can create a pleasing natural effect. Informal plantings generally have lower maintenance requirements than formal plantings.

Newly installed street trees, Columbia, Maryland neighborhood, 1973

Same view, 12 years later

Bad tree preservation practices

Preserving Trees

Regardless of size, most trees are worth saving. During a project's land planning phase, the first step is to note the areas of trees to be preserved. Plans should reflect these "tree-save" areas. It is generally easier to preserve larger groups of trees than individual or isolated trees. The latter is possible, but requires more care. In site planning for individual homes or buildings, careful siting of buildings also can help to save trees. Several techniques and principles are outlined below that can help ensure the survival of retained trees.

Inventory and documentation. It is generally recommended that a licensed arborist or landscape architect inventory and assess trees to be preserved. The inventory information should include the species, size, and condition or health of the trees and recommended action, if any, to preserve the trees. For large wooded sites, taking an inventory of groups of trees rather than individual trees is sufficient and more cost effective. The range of maintenance actions that ensure tree survival might include pruning, root pruning, deep-root fertilizing, deep-root watering, cabling, or lightning protection.

Protective fences. Before site preparation begins, protective fences (such as durable wooden snow fences or chain link fences) should be installed around all tree-save areas. Fences should remain upright and intact until all construction activity is complete. Tree preservation area signs should be affixed to the protective fences to be clearly visible from all angles of the construction site. The signs will help inform contractors and subcontractors of the importance and seriousness of tree preservation.

Construction monitoring and field control. To be successful, a tree preservation program should be carefully monitored in the field and strictly enforced. Some owners and land developers have included penalties or fines in their general contractors' construction specifications for damage or destruction of trees resulting from contractor negligence.

Activities that are detrimental to existing trees and that should be strictly prohibited include the following:

- placing backfill in tree-save areas where not indicated by the grading plan;
- felling trees into tree-save areas;
- driving construction equipment into or through tree-save areas;
- burning in or near tree-save areas;
- stacking or storing supplies in tree-save areas;
- changing site grades, which can cause drainage to flow into or to collect in tree-save areas;
- conducting trenching operations in the vicinity of trees;
- grading in the vicinity of trees;
- routing pedestrian traffic in or through tree-save areas; and
- causing physical damage to a tree.

Examples of good tree preservation practices

Postconstruction cleanup and maintenance. Following construction, all protective fences, debris, and surplus construction materials should be removed in a manner that will not damage trees. All disturbed ground areas should be seeded, sodded, or refurbished as soon as possible. Recommended tree maintenance, such as pruning, watering, or fertilizing, should likewise be implemented.

Streetscapes and Site Furniture

The streetscape within a residential neighborhood is perhaps the most visible part of the community. The streetscape helps determine the prospective home buyer's first impression of the community and reinforces the neighborhood's structure. Important to visitor and resident alike, the streetscape includes all of the elements that are visible from the street, within public rights-of-way, and within private front yards. All streetscape elements should be considered in relationship to one another. The most pleasant streetscapes are those in which all of the elements harmonize, with no single element dominating the scene.

Site furniture includes such items as benches, trash receptacles, bicycle racks, and bus shelters. Generally, there should be a unified family of fixtures within a residential neighborhood or community, and the style should be compatible with the residential buildings.

Site furniture should be selected for durability and ease of maintenance. The program and theme for a particular community will help determine the amount and placement of site furniture; in any case, site furniture should be adequately provided in pedestrian circulation areas. The following are some tips for designing streetscapes and selecting and placing site furniture.

THE FAR SIDE   By GARY LARSON

" And now, Randy, by use of song, the male sparrow will stake out his territory . . . an instinct common in the lowest animals."

Walls and Fences. Walls and fences provide screening and delineate outdoor spaces. Their design must be considered in the context of the homes they serve. Walls and fences should be viewed as an extension of the neighborhood architecture and should not compete visually with residential buildings.

Walls and fences should not be used where they interfere with a prominent view or where properties visually extend beyond the property lines. They should be used sensitively when adjacent to adjoining open space. Plantings should always be considered an integral part of any wall and fence scheme.

Street Lighting. Street lights within a residential neighborhood provide both security and aesthetic benefits. A coordinated street lighting design can help unify and distinguish a neighborhood or community. A qualified lighting consultant should be engaged to develop a lighting design. Generally, a good lighting design will:

- provide a system of maximum lighting efficiency (uniform light distribution with control of stray light and glare);
- provide continuity of lighting with a family of compatible lighting fixtures throughout the entire neighborhood or community, using accents or highlights only in places of special interest; and
- provide adequate visibility, safety, and protection.

Use lighting equipment that has an aesthetic relationship to the surrounding residential architecture during daylight hours and that is compatible with the natural landscape. Good lighting equipment will provide durability, economical operation, and convenient maintenance.

Signs. A well-designed and integrated sign system can help direct, orient, identify, and inform. A well-conceived sign system also serves as a marketing tool by establishing a recognizable neighborhood image. Generally, the following principles apply to a coordinated neighborhood sign program:

Clear signage

- Signs should complement the architecture; they should be constructed of high-quality material, and all signs should meet state specifications, local codes, and safety regulations.

- Signs should display clear and concise messages. Directional signs should reinforce an efficient flow of vehicular and pedestrian traffic.

- Signs oriented to vehicular traffic should be legible to drivers.

- Signs should not obstruct driver or pedestrian sight lines. Directional signs should be located far enough in advance of decision points to allow time for appropriate maneuvers.

- Signs should be installed only where needed. The number of signs should be kept to a minimum to avoid visual clutter.

Example of clustered mailboxes in a kiosk

Utility Boxes and Mailboxes. Above-ground utility boxes such as transformers or utility pedestals should be located and appropriately painted to minimize visual impact on the street scene. Landscape screening can also help minimize impact. However, utility companies' predetermined policies or criteria for utility box placement sometimes thwart attempts to locate boxes inconspicuously. Close coordination with utility company representatives is always required and should not be overlooked.

Many areas of the country now require the use of cluster mailboxes, which the U.S. Postal Service terms NDCBUs (neighborhood delivery and collection box units). The postal service often assists in determining the location of the NDCBU and installs the unit on a concrete pad provided by the developer. This approach works successfully for both single-family and multifamily neighborhoods. In neighborhoods with the lowest residential densities, curbside mailboxes may be considered; if so, they should respect design, color scheme, and locational criteria.

Clustered curbside mailboxes

Selling the Land Plan

For a residential neighborhood land plan to be successful, it must be salable. Many developers and builders still think that selling begins when and only when model homes open for business – and that selling ends immediately after the last home is sold. Actually, selling begins during the site analysis phase of the land planning process and continues long after the residential neighborhood is occupied. The following tips will help you sell land plans and communities to local decision makers and other affected parties.

Do your homework.

Do your homework. Investigate market trends and undertake market research, making sure that you do not pay too much for the land at the outset. Define a clear set of objectives you wish to achieve.

Get organized.

Get organized. Devise a sales strategy at the local level, where it will have the greatest impact. Do not hesitate to call on specialists from outside your region for help with specific problems.

Believe in what you are selling. Get excited about your land plan. Use eye-catching graphic exhibits, examples, and comparative studies to help sell your concepts (see Figure 4.5). Present positive solutions and back them up with examples and expert testimony.

Promote and market your program.

Promote and market your program. Understand the advantages of what you are selling and promote your program's attributes to your banker, realtor, planning staff, and local politicians and civic groups. Do not wait for criticism to put you on the defensive.

Selling often is a reiterative process. Keep selling, and do not give up. Often you must recommend changes to existing regulations or model ordinances to support innovative forms of development.

Ensure customer satisfaction. Remember that customer satisfaction and service are important ingredients for continued success. As a developer or builder, your reputation is only as good as your last residential community.

Ensure customer satisfaction.

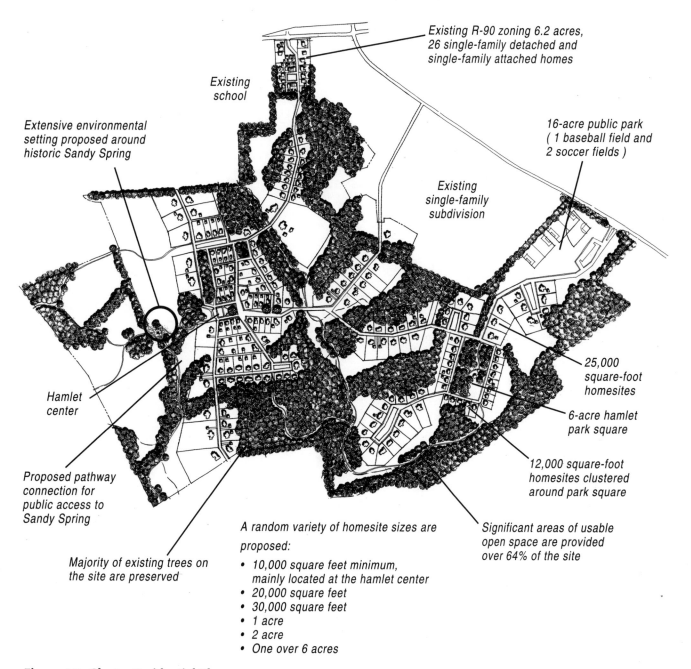

Existing R-90 zoning 6.2 acres, 26 single-family detached and single-family attached homes

Existing school

Extensive environmental setting proposed around historic Sandy Spring

16-acre public park (1 baseball field and 2 soccer fields)

Existing single-family subdivision

Hamlet center

25,000 square-foot homesites

6-acre hamlet park square

12,000 square-foot homesites clustered around park square

Proposed pathway connection for public access to Sandy Spring

Majority of existing trees on the site are preserved

A random variety of homesite sizes are proposed:
- 10,000 square feet minimum, mainly located at the hamlet center
- 20,000 square feet
- 30,000 square feet
- 1 acre
- 2 acre
- One over 6 acres

Significant areas of usable open space are provided over 64% of the site

Figure 4.5 Cluster Residential Plan

Prepared by LDR International, Inc., Andres Duany and Elizabeth Plater-Zyberk, and printed with permission of Joseph Alfandre & Company, Inc. and Potomac Investment Associates.

Designing with Neighborhood Amenities

In this chapter:

- Natural Amenities
- Created Amenities
- Planning the Amenity Package
- Creating a Sense of Place
- Designing a Model Home Sales Area

Open space can be an amenity.

Who would not select the home with a spectacular view, a lakeside setting, or access to a community park? In today's highly competitive housing markets, developers and builders who offer an outstanding amenity package enjoy a decided edge. Amenities can:

- enhance a project's image;
- increase real estate values;
- provide leverage for rezoning decisions;
- add marketing advantage;
- make use of undevelopable land; and
- create a social focus for a community.

Before prospective home buyers even look at a house, they must be convinced that the neighborhood is a fitting place to live. People buy into a community and a lifestyle; they do not just buy a house. Nonetheless, affordability remains the ultimate amenity for the home buyer. That is why it is important to keep the cost of neighborhood and site amenities in perspective. Knowing how to design with amenities and make them work to your advantage is an important part of the housing affordability equation.

Neighborhood and site amenities can be natural or created. Natural amenities capitalize on existing physical features of the site, while created amenities are built into the development during project planning and implementation. Many created amenities do not add significantly to the cost of planning or construction, and some can even save money.

Both amenity types can make an important contribution to successful project image building and marketing. The development team must carefully weigh the costs and benefits of each proposed amenity and make every effort to match the amenity to the target market.

Natural Amenities

One of the single biggest mistakes made by many developers over the years has been the failure to take advantage of natural amenities. Too often, development industry professionals have viewed natural site features as obstacles to optimum land use. To the contrary, natural site resources present a challenge to, not a constraint on, creative land planning. A site's natural features such as vegetation, hedgerows, specimen trees, woodlots, varied topography, slopes, rock outcroppings, drainage ways, wetlands, streams, ponds, and lakes frequently cannot be replaced at any cost – and they add unparalleled interest to the site.

Early in the development process, it is essential to identify the unique and desirable features of the site to be preserved as well as those that must be left untouched to comply with environmental regulations. Urban foresters, landscape architects, ecologists, and other professionals can help analyze a site's natural features and guide preliminary

design decisions. The development program can then be matched to the land resources and the target market.

Created Amenities

Created amenities are added to the site during the development process and can generally be grouped into three categories: planning amenities, recreation amenities, and image amenities.

Planning amenities can be incorporated into a community through creative layout and design of the site. Clustering of homes, solar orientation, open space networks, and view corridors are examples of planning amenities.

Planning amenities

Recreation amenities are features that residents use during their leisure time. Most high-cost amenities – club houses or swimming pools, golf courses, marinas, tennis courts, etc. – fall into this category. But opportunities abound to create affordable recreation amenities as well. Children's playlots, community garden plots, jogging or exercise trails, and picnic shelters and barbeques can be provided at little cost and require minimal land area.

Image amenities provide the developer with the opportunity to create a special community identity. Image amenities may seem less tangible than recreation amenities, but they can set a development apart from the competition and convey to potential homeowners that the community is a special place to live. Image amenities can include:

Recreation amenities

- entrance landscaping;
- graphic identity used on entrance signs and in marketing materials;
- roadway landscaping;
- special street lights and accent lighting;
- decorative fences at property perimeters and major intersections;
- attractive site furniture; and
- clustered mailboxes under shelter in a landscaped setting.

Design guidelines and restrictive covenants that ensure design consistency in architecture, site improvements, and landscaping are also considered image amenities. Even though such requirements have no outward manifestation when a development is new, prospective buyers understand the importance of the requirements in protecting property values and maintaining community image over the long term.

Image amenities

Planning the Amenity Package

Natural amenities may be as simple as a specimen tree or as complex as an extensive wetlands ecosystem. The developer should capitalize on the following natural features:

Woodlands. Retain and preserve as much existing vegetation as possible. Wooded lots, lots with wooded edges, and even lots with a few mature specimen trees command premiums over treeless lots. Wooded open space adds beauty and variety to passive recreation areas. The cost of preserving mature trees is often less than a typical landscape budget.

Hedgerows. Retain significant trees while carefully and selectively clearing the undergrowth. Hedgerows can separate areas and different product types, screen adjacent uses, and add value to homesites.

Topography and slopes. Use variation in the terrain to maximize solar orientation, develop walk-out units, and separate different product types. Steep slopes that must remain undeveloped can add character to open space through strategic placement of trails and overlooks.

Rock outcroppings. Incorporate outcroppings into open spaces and at entrances and focal intersections. It is advisable to use rock outcroppings in a way that closely resembles how they would appear in nature.

Water bodies. Maximize both the public and private views of streams, rivers, ponds, and lakes. If possible, provide water access for active recreation use using piers, pedestrian walks, small boat ramps, or even small sand beaches.

Wetlands and other sensitive areas. The presence of environmentally sensitive lands or features provides developers with the opportunity to make a public statement in favor of environmental protection. That statement, in turn, can become the centerpiece of the marketing campaign. Developers can promote an environmentally sound plan as leverage for greater citizen support, expedited approvals, or the implementation of performance standards. Requirements for the provision of stream buffers and wildlife corridors and for the protection of wetlands, tidal marshes, steep slopes, and trees are environmental obstacles that can be transformed into community assets.

Existing structures. While not strictly natural features, existing structures such as barns or building ruins such as stone foundations often can be included in an affordable amenity package.

In planning an amenity package, developers and builders should consider the following principles:

Match the amenities to the market. A common mistake among developers and builders is to fail to match the site amenities to the target market (see Figure 5.1). For instance, in a project aimed at retirees and the elderly, a daycare facility for children may not be the most appropriate amenity for the community. Does a market exist for the particular amenity you are considering? Can buyers in that market afford the amenities you are planning to offer?

Simple, Cost-Effective Amenities for Basic Markets	**Mid-Range, More Costly Amenities for Middle Markets**	**Most Costly Amenities for Upscale Markets**
Putting green	Golf learning center, pay-for-play municipal golf course	Signature golf course, private country club
Trees	More trees	Significant number of large transplanted trees, arboretum
Horse fence	Simple barn and paddock	Equestrian center
Entrance sign	Entrance feature	Gatehouse or other elaborate entry feature
Garden plots, wildflower seeding	Annual and perennial flower gardens	Greenhouse or garden center
Access to waterfront	Pier, boat launch or dock	Marina
Pedestrian trail	Pedestrian pathway with simple bridges, vita course	Pedestrian walkway, promenade, bridges, gazebos, and overlooks
Views	Views of open space	Scenic amenity views
Selectively located fences	Fences and walls	Stone or brick walls
Picnic benches	Picnic shelter	Community park and recreation facilities
Selective placement of street lights at entrance or key intersections	Street lighting throughout	Street lighting throughout and accent lighting
Unified mailboxes	Cluster mailboxes	Mail kiosks
Cross country ski trails	Skating pond or rink	Ski slopes, resort
Open field	Playlots and recreation areas, swimming pool	Health and fitness center
Preserved foundation remnants	Restored barn	Restored historic structure as community center
Sand volleyball area	Multipurpose play courts	Tennis courts
Stormwater retention pond	Water feature	Water feature with retention, moving water, fountains, or waterfall
Natural wetlands	Enhanced wetlands	Wetlands, natural areas with interpretive trails and boardwalks
Barbeque grills	Stone fireplace	Dining facilities in community center
Hedgerow	Decorative planting	Elaborate thematic planting scheme
Rock outcropping	Stone walls	Sculpture garden rock fabrication
Benches	Decks and gazebos	Amphitheater

Figure 5.1 Match the Amenities to the Market

Balance the amenity's function and its location to ensure marketing advantage. This principle is one of the keys to the successful design of neighborhood amenities. At the outset, you must understand the technical requirements of the amenities you are planning, particularly when elaborate and costly features such as a golf course, marina, or health and fitness center are under consideration. It is essential to seek the advice of competent specialists early in the planning process. Once you have selected a particular amenity or amenity package, you must make certain that your development is designed to maximize the value of the amenity. In other words, the amenity must be visible to potential buyers and should be located for optimum homesite frontage and views. Further, it is important to remember that most amenity features serve a dual function (for example, recreation and open space, water feature and stormwater management, activity feature and view).

In most cases, the land planning team arrives at the best solution for satisfying all development objectives through a give-and-take process. When designing amenity features, developers must consider alternative layout plans as discussed in chapter 3 (see Figures 5.2 and 5.3). In the case of a golf course community, for example, the course architect may be asked to revise the course layout to satisfy the developer's desire to create more homesites with views of the course. On the other hand, a developer might be well advised to relocate a few homesites to allow a public view of the golf course from a main entrance road.

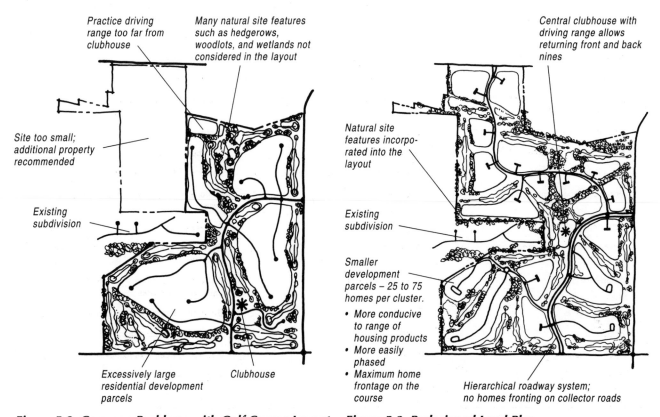

Figure 5.2 Common Problems with Golf Course Layout   Figure 5.3 Redesigned Land Plan

Provide amenities that offer year-round advantage. An amenity that is successful in one geographic region may be problematic in another due to seasonal use patterns, water requirements, or consumer preferences. Provide seasonal balance in your amenity package by considering the following tips:

- Provide sheltered or covered outdoor recreation spaces that extend the outdoor recreation season.

- Provide indoor as well as outdoor recreation amenities.

- Make sure that amenities are designed to present an attractive appearance during the "off" season.

- Use landscaping that provides unusual seasonal color or texture. For instance, in colder climates select a particular plant that provides interest in snow. The same principle can be applied to a desert location.

- Incorporate evergreen plant material to provide year-round color and texture.

- In temperate climates with extended winters, site graphics and sign programs can introduce accent colors and interest.

Use of fencing and wildflower plantings enhances a community entrance.

Balance the amenity's costs and benefits. Developers must thoroughly analyze all the financial aspects of a residential neighborhood, including the costs and benefits of the amenity package. Though often overlooked, consideration of amenity costs and benefits demands answers to the following questions:

- Are the amenity's initial construction costs affordable?

- What is the cost of the land that must be set aside for the amenity? Is it affordable?

- Are the initial construction costs and the carrying costs on the debt associated with the amenity offset by the value added to the homes?

- Can the amenity be phased over time to minimize up-front construction costs?

- Have the amenity package's operating and maintenance costs been evaluated?

Figure 5.4 illustrates average initial expenditures for some of the more popular amenities.

Estimated Averages for Type of Amenity (Initial Cost)

Open Space Enhancement
- Tree preservation/edge treatment (1/4 mile) $17,000
- Reforestation (1 acre) $15,000
- Wildflower seeding (1 acre) $2,500

Pathways/Jogging Trails (1-mile long x 6-feet wide)
- Crushed limestone $24,000
- Asphalt $55,000
- Concrete $90,000

Fitness Course (10 stations) $6,500

Wood Dock (80 square feet) $3,000
Wood Pedestrian Bridge (12-feet long) $3,000

Wood Deck (1,000 square feet)$12,000

Play Fields/Courts
- Tennis (two court) $45,000
- Basketball $15,000
- Softball field $15,000
- Soccer/multipurpose field $18,000
- Sand volleyball court $2,500

Children's Playlot (30 x 35 feet with play equipment) $20,000

Community Garden Plots (land only)

Site Furnishings
- Picnic table $500
- Bench $600
- Fences
  - Wood board (500 linear feet) $22,000
  - Split rail (500 linear feet) $9,000
- Gazebo $8,000

18-Hole Golf Course $2,700,000 to $4,500,000
- Golf club house $100 per square foot
- Maintenance equipment and building $500,000

Figure 5.4 Costs for Some Popular Amenities

Consider long-term operating and maintenance implications. Developers must formulate a workable plan for transferring amenity features to a long-term operating and ownership entity, particularly in the case of sophisticated features such as golf courses, marinas, tennis courts, and health and fitness clubs. Yet, developers must also make provision for the ownership and control of common open space. A frequent solution is to establish a cluster, community, or homeowners association (HOA) that assumes ownership of common open space. Information on the mechanics of establishing and operating such an association is available from the Community Associations Institute.

As an alternative to an HOA, it may be possible in certain situations to convey all the property to individual property owners, with deed restrictions, easements, or covenants attached to the open space to ensure its future protection. In some cases, it may also be advantageous to convey the amenity to a municipal, county, state, or federal agency or land trust for ownership and continued maintenance. Again, developers must carefully weigh these factors to ensure that the long-range operating and maintenance responsibility remains consistent with the community's marketing objectives.

Creating a Sense of Place

How do planners and designers create a theme for a neighborhood or community when the site offers little interest? How do developers create a sense of place or a feeling of a special destination? The following principles provide some guidance on designing with created amenities:

Create a theme. Create a distinctive theme to distinguish a prospective neighborhood from all others. It is usually advisable to build on a theme indigenous to the area by incorporating a local, historical, or cultural tradition. It is also possible to transpose a theme from another geographic region, although such an approach usually requires greater care and a meticulous concern for detail and authenticity. The theme should be reinforced by the architectural style, color palette, site details, landscaping plan, and site graphics program as well as by the name of the community.

Carefully locate manmade amenities. Orchestrate the placement of manmade amenity features for greatest marketing advantage. The buildings and amenities with the highest impact should be located on the most strategic and visible parcels of land to transform the parcels into community focal points and orientation features. For example, it is usually best to place the club house or community recreation center near the entrance to the neighborhood to emphasize strategic viewing.

Design a unique landscape. Design and create an exciting and unique landscape where none previously existed. Creating a unique landscape may require major artistic manipulation to develop a genuine setting that looks as if it always existed. Be careful, however, not to allow the design to become so trite or contrived that it looks out of place.

Use dominant architecture. Adopt a more dominant architectural style. This is contrary to the usual practice of designing for a site distinguished by great natural beauty, which calls for more understated architecture. Even though the architecture on a featureless site automatically becomes more dominant, an indigenous architectural style usually works best.

Design distinctive site graphics. Design a distinctive, high-quality system of site graphics to help create and emphasize the new sense of place. The graphic system and project logo should be reinforced by the project's print graphics.

Gazebo or bus shelter should be designed to reinforce distinctive architectural theme.

Distinctive site graphics program

Designing a Model Home Sales Area

If you have a product to sell, you should create the best possible "package" or environment in which to market and sell that product. The following are some principles to consider in designing your model homes and the sales area.

Generally, it is advisable to locate model homes and the sales center on the most highly valued piece of property within the community. By showcasing the model homes and the sales center, developers can put their best foot forward and, at the same time, retain the model homes for sale at project buildout when greater premiums can be charged.

In locating model homes, it is important keep the public entrance and circulation separate from construction traffic, if possible. In larger scale neighborhoods or communities where several builders may be constructing homes, builders should collectively create a model home park, street of dreams, or parade of homes that offers one-stop shopping. Locating the model homes close to such recreation features as tennis courts, pools, play areas, club houses, or parks helps ensure maximum visibility of amenities (see Figures 5.5 and 5.6).

In the case of model units within a townhome or multifamily community, it is generally preferable to develop a small building group as the model. The smaller building will be easier to manage and maintain, eliminates the distractions of operating the models in proximity to for-sale (or sold) units, and offers an intimacy of scale that can be lost if the models are set in a larger building group. Generally, a 4- to 6-unit building is preferable to a 10-unit building. Also, orientation of the building is important. To the extent possible, the entrances, patios, or balconies of the models should be oriented to the south to take full advantage of the sun.

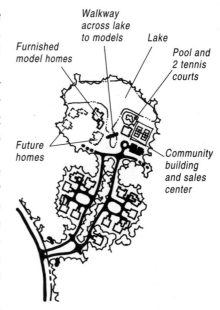

Figure 5.5 Typical Layout Plan for Model Home and Sales Area

Figure 5.6 Summerlake, Fredericksburg, Virginia

A home in a typical model home park

Source: LDR International, Inc.

A word of caution is in order about the construction of models. In the case of new or untested products, developers may wish to build untested units on the least desirable portion of the site to ensure that all problems are worked out. Any architectural and design modifications can be made when units are constructed as model homes on the community's prime site.

With the general location of the model homes and sales center determined, it is important to develop a thoughtful and creative site design plan. The following specific design items should guide development of the site plan for the model homes and sales area:

Convenient and adequate parking. Parking areas should be located to provide a clear approach to the homes from a distance or angle that accentuates the most exciting site and architectural features. Temporary parking lots, on-street parking, and the delayed construction of driveways can create an enhanced sense of openness and space (see Figure 5.7).

Good pedestrian circulation. Walkways must be sufficiently wide (greater than three to four feet) to allow ease of pedestrian circulation among the model homes. Generally, curving walks are the best solution for easy circulation. The choice between curved versus straight walks should relate to the design of the homes and the landscape treatment. In any case, rather than forcing circulation too close to the homes, the walkways should permit prospective home buyers to step back and fully view and appreciate the architecture and the overall community design (see Figure 5.8). As for pavement material, stepping stones, bricks, or pavers are attractive and can be easily removed when the model units are sold.

Convenient benches. Benches should be located to allow people to sit and contemplate their potential purchase. Fences, plantings, and earth forms can be effectively used to direct people to and between homes and back through the sales office.

Signs. A distinctive site graphics system should be developed for the sales center sign, directional signs, and model home identification signs. The system should be consistent with the overall community identity and sign program. Pedestrian lighting and accent lighting of the units is especially important and can enhance nighttime selling.

Patio treatment. The relationship of indoor to outdoor spaces in model homes is particularly important, especially with today's smaller homes. Special outdoor features can include benches, barbecues, attractive paving materials, water features, sculpture, decks, or trellises. Varied outdoor treatments for several model homes can illustrate a range of options from the basic package provided by the builder to a luxurious patio or garden area. In the model as in the development, however, remember to match the level of options with the lifestyle expectations of the target market.

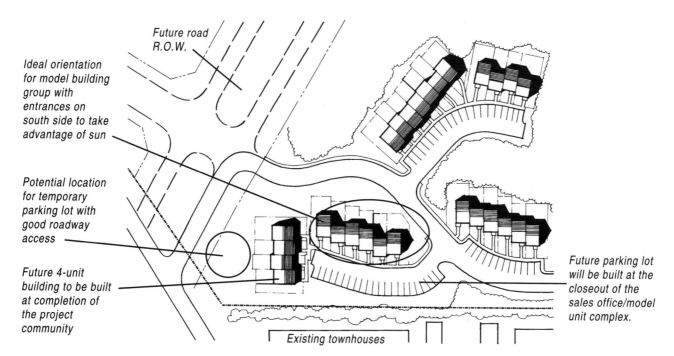

Future road R.O.W.

Ideal orientation for model building group with entrances on south side to take advantage of sun

Potential location for temporary parking lot with good roadway access

Future 4-unit building to be built at completion of the project community

Future parking lot will be built at the closeout of the sales office/model unit complex.

Existing townhouses

Figure 5.7   *Engineered Site Plan – Ultimate Layout*

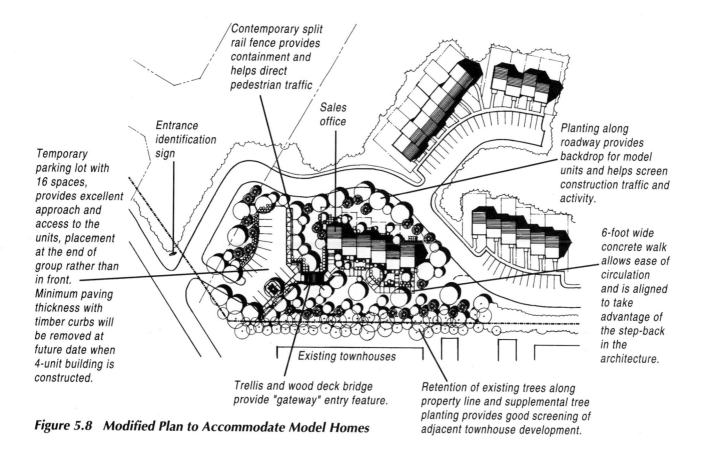

Contemporary split rail fence provides containment and helps direct pedestrian traffic

Sales office

Entrance identification sign

Temporary parking lot with 16 spaces, provides excellent approach and access to the units, placement at the end of group rather than in front.
Minimum paving thickness with timber curbs will be removed at future date when 4-unit building is constructed.

Planting along roadway provides backdrop for model units and helps screen construction traffic and activity.

6-foot wide concrete walk allows ease of circulation and is aligned to take advantage of the step-back in the architecture.

Existing townhouses

Trellis and wood deck bridge provide "gateway" entry feature.

Retention of existing trees along property line and supplemental tree planting provides good screening of adjacent townhouse development.

Figure 5.8   *Modified Plan to Accommodate Model Homes*

Landsaver Design Patterns

In this chapter:

- Single-Family Detached Homes
- Single-Family Attached Homes
- Multifamily Stacked and Attached Homes
- Mixed Residential Product Types

The landsaver design patterns on the following pages reflect the latest and most up-to-date approaches to site planning. They illustrate a range of housing types and densities from single-family detached to multi-family homes. The housing types respond to various land forms and take advantage of a range of regional architectural styles. The patterns are presented in three-dimensional form as well as in plan view. All illustrations were generated by a Computer-Aided Drafting and Design (CADD) system, which offers tremendous capability for visual simulation and modeling.

One word of caution is in order in using the patterns. Developers and builders should not simply "cut and paste" the patterns. Rather, they should use the landsaver design patterns in light of the design principles outlined in the preceding chapters. Developers and builders should choose their patterns carefully to make sure that the layouts:

- respond to land constraints;
- reflect market realities; and
- lend themselves to artful integration with other clusters to create a unified land plan.

Single-Family Detached Homes

1. Low-Density Detached Homes

Even with relatively low-density single-family detached homes, cluster development patterns can be incorporated into the land plan. Lower overall density makes it possible to adapt a cluster, cul-de-sac, or turn-around street pattern to a variety of land forms that respect sensitive environmental features.

Home Type	Street	Approximate Net Density (Homes per acre)	Topography	Special Considerations
Single-family detached	Public or private; can easily accommodate open swale drainage sections	2.75	Flat, rolling or steep land	Adapts to a wide range of situations and topographic conditions; works in wooded or unwooded settings

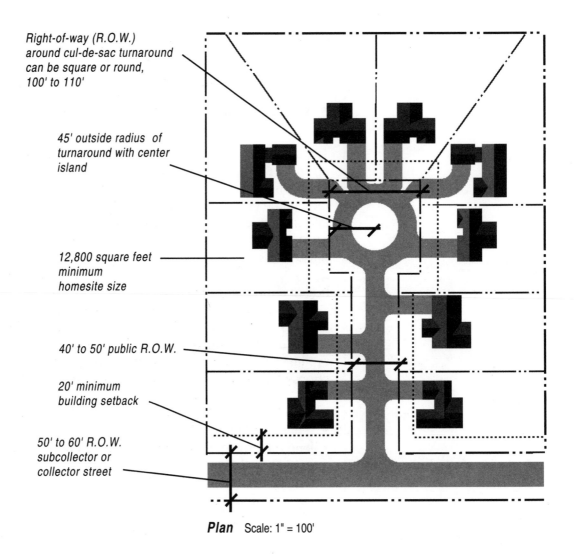

Right-of-way (R.O.W.) around cul-de-sac turnaround can be square or round, 100' to 110'

45' outside radius of turnaround with center island

12,800 square feet minimum homesite size

40' to 50' public R.O.W.

20' minimum building setback

50' to 60' R.O.W. subcollector or collector street

Plan   Scale: 1" = 100'

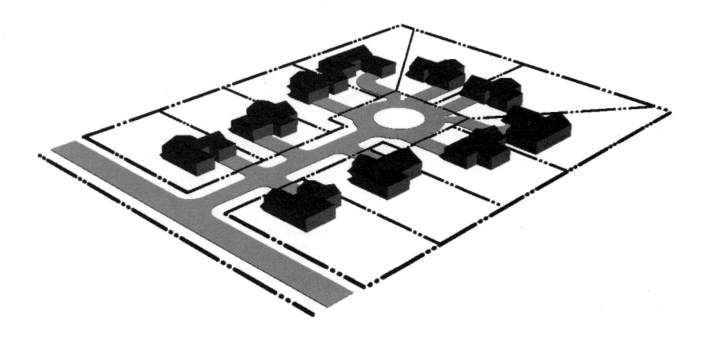

Existing trees should
be preserved where
possible. New tree
planting is recom-
mended on
unwooded sites.

Sidewalks are generally
not needed in low-density
situations.

Road can be public
or private.

This density can
easily accommodate
open swale sections.

2. Medium-Density Detached Homes

The medium-density cluster, cul-de-sac, or turn-around street pattern is one of the most prevalent patterns in suburban communities. It is relatively cost-efficient and can be replicated easily. Its repeated use over large areas without significant open space has drawn some criticism from community planners and traditionalists. If sensitively used, however, this pattern can contribute to a successful land plan.

Home Type	Street	Approximate Net Density (Homes per acre)	Topography	Special Considerations
Single-family detached	Public or private, but public streets predominate	3.5 to 4.0	Flat or rolling land is preferable, but houses can be constructed on steep land if space between clusters is provided to allow for gradient changes	Adapts to a wide range of situations, particularly if streets are short and setbacks are varied; street tree planting and landscaping are essential

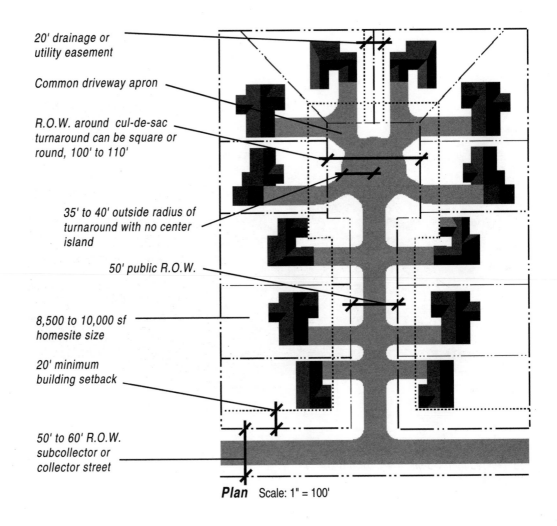

20' drainage or utility easement

Common driveway apron

R.O.W. around cul-de-sac turnaround can be square or round, 100' to 110'

35' to 40' outside radius of turnaround with no center island

50' public R.O.W.

8,500 to 10,000 sf homesite size

20' minimum building setback

50' to 60' R.O.W. subcollector or collector street

Plan   Scale: 1" = 100'

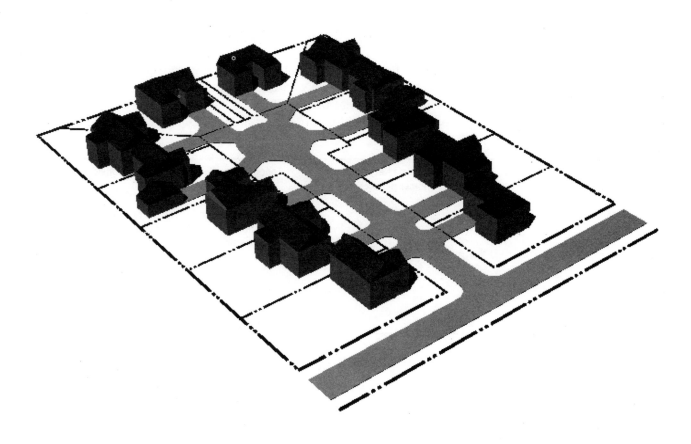

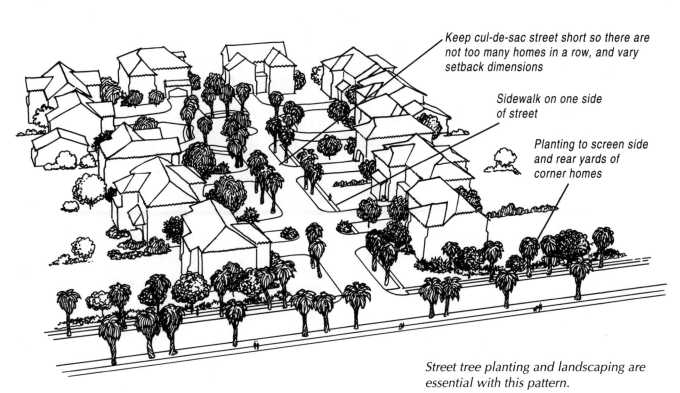

Keep cul-de-sac street short so there are not too many homes in a row, and vary setback dimensions

Sidewalk on one side of street

Planting to screen side and rear yards of corner homes

Street tree planting and landscaping are essential with this pattern.

3. Detached "Eyebrow" Homes

This configuration is a variation of the cul-de-sac scheme. It can be used effectively to create a sense of place or special identity within a neighborhood that uses multiple patterns. Another benefit is that it eliminates individual driveways along a residential collector street.

Home Type	Street	Approximate Net Density (Homes per acre)	Topography	Special Considerations
Single-family detached	Public or private	3.5 to 4.0	Flat or rolling land is preferable, but houses with walk-out basements can be developed on steep land; space between clusters must be provided to allow for gradient changes	Adapts to a wide range of situations; various forms and configurations of eyebrows can be used in combination with other cluster patterns to provide variety and interest

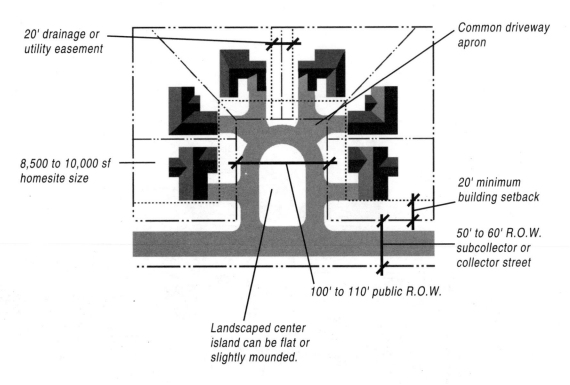

20' drainage or utility easement

Common driveway apron

8,500 to 10,000 sf homesite size

20' minimum building setback

50' to 60' R.O.W. subcollector or collector street

100' to 110' public R.O.W.

Landscaped center island can be flat or slightly mounded.

Plan   Scale: 1" = 100'

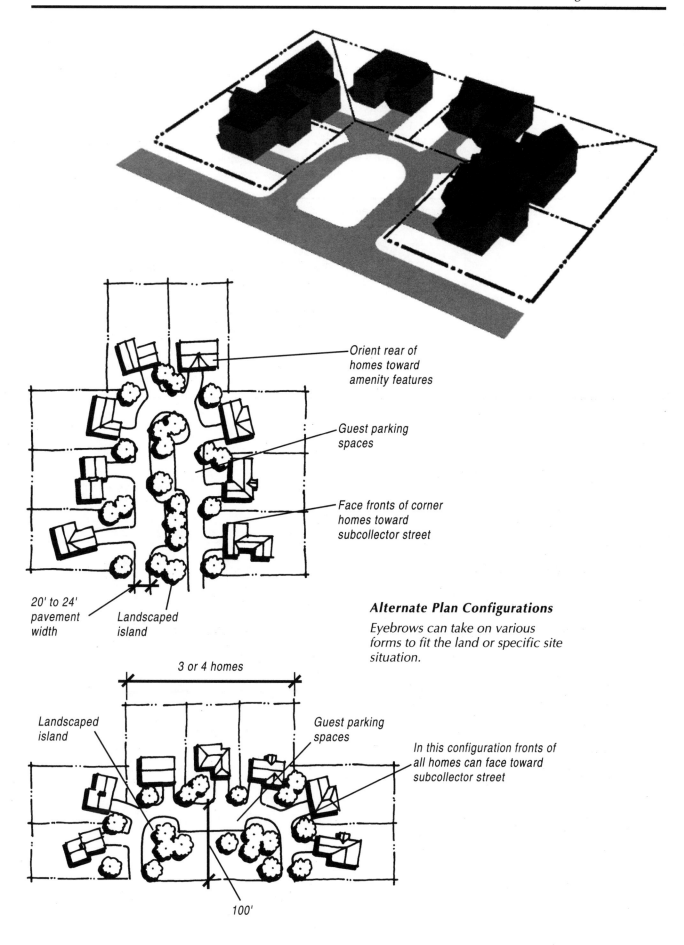

Orient rear of homes toward amenity features

Guest parking spaces

Face fronts of corner homes toward subcollector street

20' to 24' pavement width

Landscaped island

Alternate Plan Configurations

Eyebrows can take on various forms to fit the land or specific site situation.

3 or 4 homes

Landscaped island

Guest parking spaces

In this configuration fronts of all homes can face toward subcollector street

100'

4. Detached Homes With Shared Driveways

A cost-effective approach suited for use along a public residential street, this pattern permits the creation of an intimate scale and a tighter cluster arrangement that is hard to achieve with public street standards. It can be used with a variety of homesite or lot sizes.

Home Type	Street	Approximate Net Density (Homes per acre)	Topography	Special Considerations
Single-family detached	Private	4.0	Flat or rolling land is preferable, but houses with walk-out basements can be developed on steep land; space between clusters must be provided to allow for gradient changes	Can be used in combination with other cluster patterns to provide variety and interest; homes require carefully integrated architectural design, grading, and site design; homeowners must assume responsibility for common maintenance and the replacement cost of shared driveways

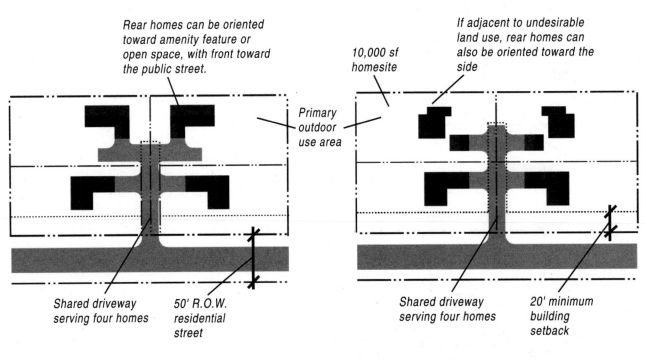

Rear homes can be oriented toward amenity feature or open space, with front toward the public street.

If adjacent to undesirable land use, rear homes can also be oriented toward the side

10,000 sf homesite

Primary outdoor use area

Shared driveway serving four homes

50' R.O.W. residential street

Shared driveway serving four homes

20' minimum building setback

Plan – Option A   Scale: 1" = 100'

Plan – Option B   Scale: 1" = 100'

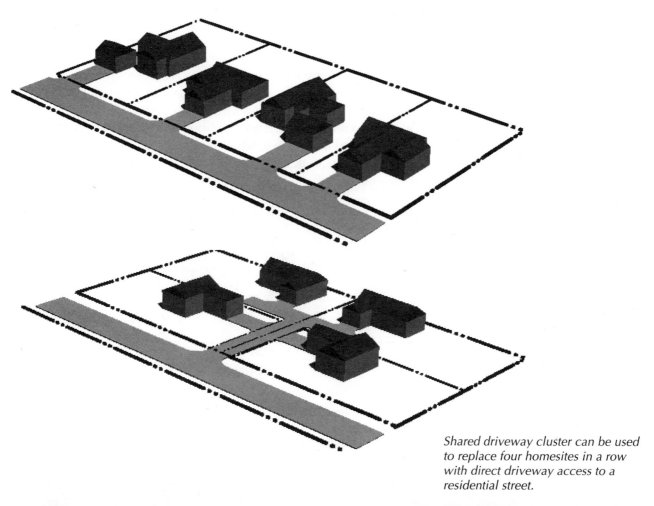

Shared driveway cluster can be used to replace four homesites in a row with direct driveway access to a residential street.

5. Detached Homes With Shared Courtyards

Recent experiments with large expensive homes on relatively small homesites (4,500 to 6,000 square feet) have succeeded in many parts of the country. The reason is a lifestyle preference for the advantages of a single-family detached home without the responsibility of owning or maintaining large-lot acreage. This type of pattern is particularly well suited to clusters in golf or recreation communities.

Home Type	Street	Approximate Net Density (Homes per acre)	Topography	Special Considerations
Single-family detached	Private	5.0 to 6.0	Flat or rolling land is preferable, but steep sites with space between clusters can accommodate courtyard homes	Requires careful architectural and site design

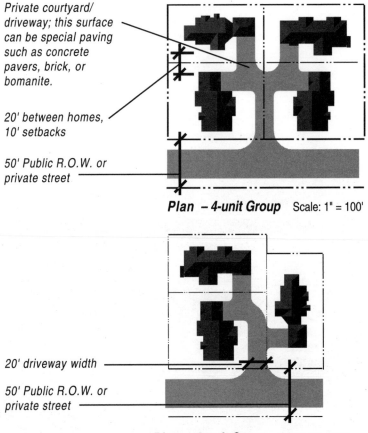

Private courtyard/ driveway; this surface can be special paving such as concrete pavers, brick, or bomanite.

20' between homes, 10' setbacks

50' Public R.O.W. or private street

Plan – 4-unit Group   Scale: 1" = 100'

20' driveway width

50' Public R.O.W. or private street

Plan – 3-unit Group   Scale: 1" = 100'

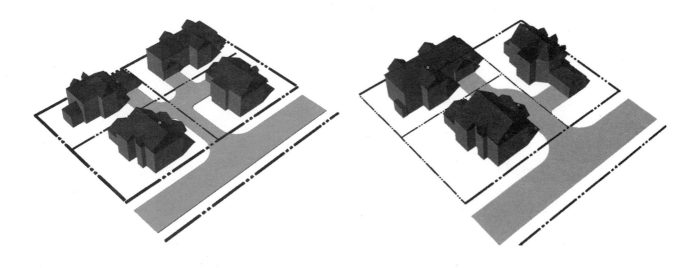

Tight clusters have been effectively used in Avenel, Potomac, Maryland.

Developers: *Potomac Investment Associates and Rocky Gorge Communities*
Architect: *Kaufman and Meeks*

6. Detached Homes With Cluster Garages

This pattern is adaptable to smaller lots, particularly when lots range from 6,000 to 8,000 square feet. A variation of the patio home concept (discussed later), this pattern permits side yards on both sides of the homes but requires placement of garages on a side property line.

Home Type	Street	Approximate Net Density (Homes per acre)	Topography	Special Considerations
Single-family detached homes with attached garages	Public or private	4.0 to 5.5	Flat or rolling land	Requires carefully integrated architectural design, grading, and site design; works best with a one-car garage per home

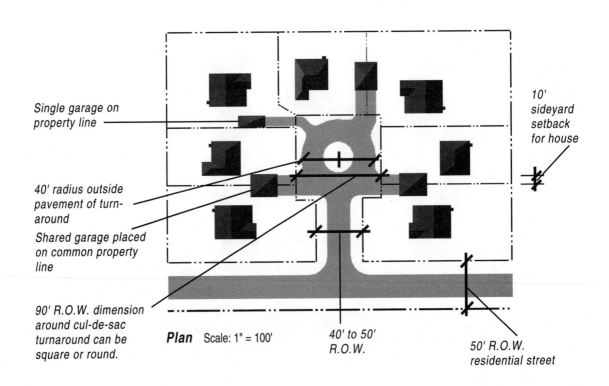

Single garage on property line

40' radius outside pavement of turn-around

Shared garage placed on common property line

90' R.O.W. dimension around cul-de-sac turnaround can be square or round.

10' sideyard setback for house

Plan   Scale: 1" = 100'

40' to 50' R.O.W.

50' R.O.W. residential street

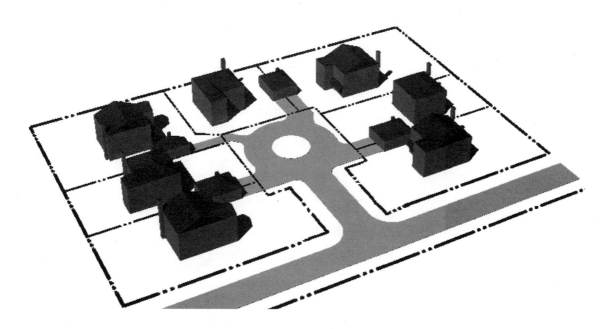

This cluster pattern was used effectively in the planning of Kindler Commons, Columbia, Maryland.

Developer: *Mark Building Company*
Land Planners: *LDR International, Inc.*

7. Detached Homes With Private Parking Courts

Although not used in most parts of the country because of local road requirements, the private parking court configuration can be particularly cost-effective. It lends itself well to small-lot development where lots range from 5,000 to 6,000 square feet. The private parking court configuration can be used for zero lot-line homes or conventional single-family detached homes with two side yards.

Home Type	Street	Approximate Net Density (Homes per acre)	Topography	Special Considerations
Single-family detached	Private	4.0 to 6.0	Flat or rolling land	Requires careful architectural and site design; landscaping is critical, especially in parking areas

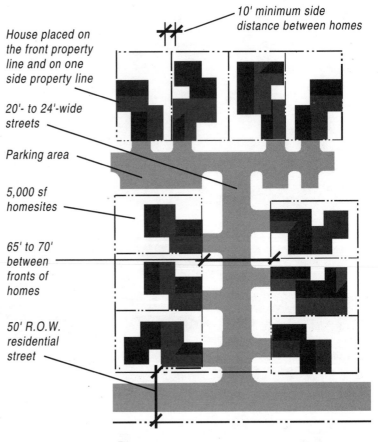

House placed on the front property line and on one side property line

10' minimum side distance between homes

20'- to 24'-wide streets

Parking area

5,000 sf homesites

65' to 70' between fronts of homes

50' R.O.W. residential street

Plan Scale: 1" = 100'

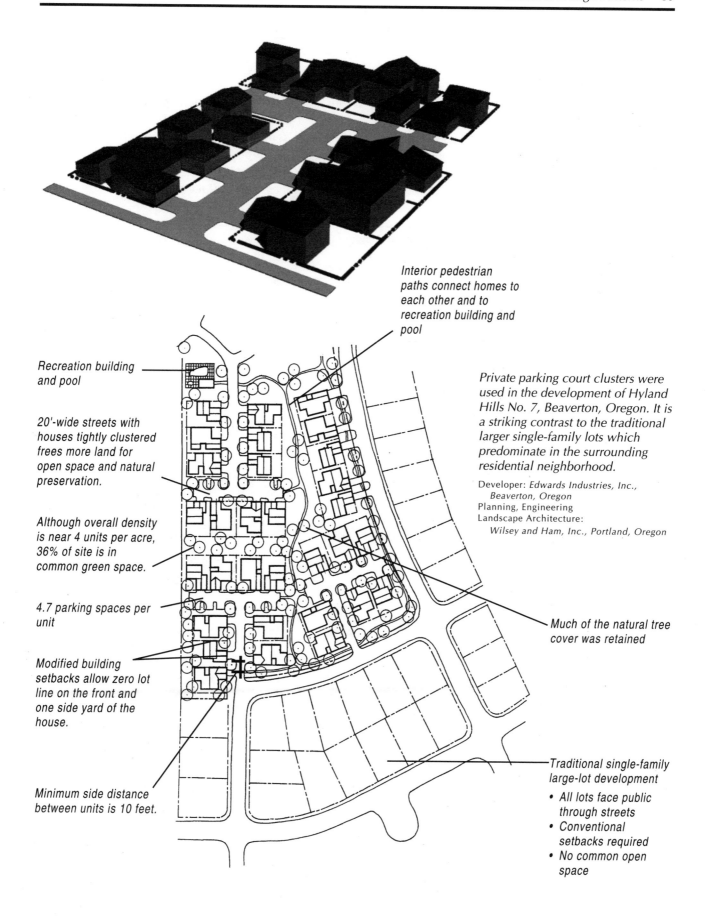

Interior pedestrian paths connect homes to each other and to recreation building and pool

Recreation building and pool

20'-wide streets with houses tightly clustered frees more land for open space and natural preservation.

Although overall density is near 4 units per acre, 36% of site is in common green space.

4.7 parking spaces per unit

Modified building setbacks allow zero lot line on the front and one side yard of the house.

Minimum side distance between units is 10 feet.

Private parking court clusters were used in the development of Hyland Hills No. 7, Beaverton, Oregon. It is a striking contrast to the traditional larger single-family lots which predominate in the surrounding residential neighborhood.

Developer: *Edwards Industries, Inc., Beaverton, Oregon*
Planning, Engineering
Landscape Architecture:
Wilsey and Ham, Inc., Portland, Oregon

Much of the natural tree cover was retained

Traditional single-family large-lot development
• All lots face public through streets
• Conventional setbacks required
• No common open space

8. Detached Homes With Commons

This approach to clustering emphasizes open space by orienting the front doors of houses to a formal common or mews. This pattern is appropriate for urban and semi-urban settings yet works well as a transitional cluster. The product type can include homes with carports or integral or separate garages. The pattern can also succeed with moderately priced basic homes with surface parking.

Home Type	Street	Approximate Net Density (Homes per acre)	Topography	Special Considerations
Single-family detached	Public or private	4.0 to 5.0	Flat or gently rolling land	Generally lends itself to more urban, formal situations; design and detailing of common space is critical

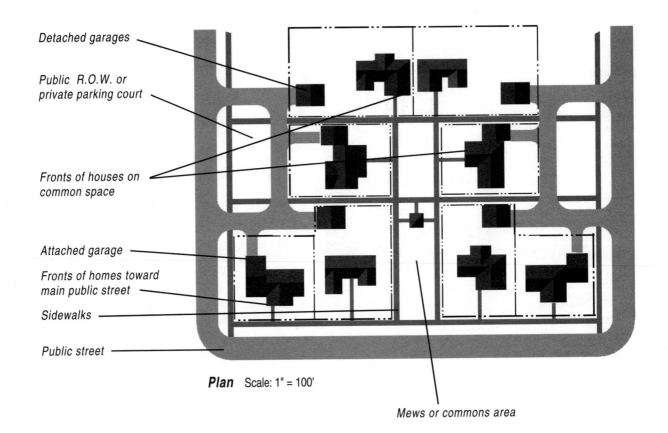

Detached garages

Public R.O.W. or private parking court

Fronts of houses on common space

Attached garage

Fronts of homes toward main public street

Sidewalks

Public street

Plan　Scale: 1" = 100'

Mews or commons area

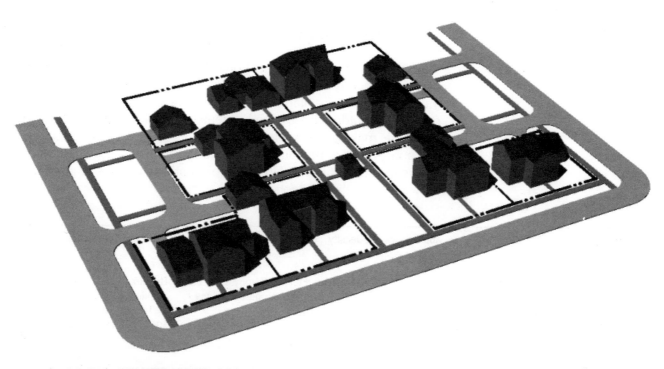

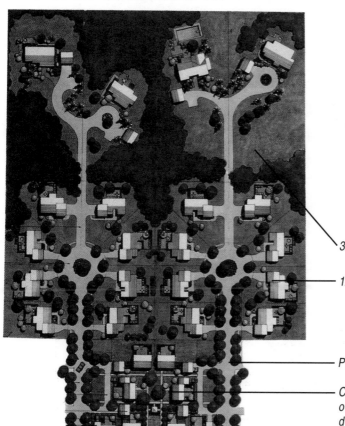

3/4- to 1-acre homesites

1/4-acre homesites

Public residential street

*Commons cluster can be used with
other cluster patterns to provide
density transition*

Main collector street

Transitional Cluster Site Plan   No Scale

9. Detached Patio Homes

The patio home or zero lot-line home is sited on or close to one of the lot's side property lines. The wall of the home that abuts the neighboring property line is blank and lacks windows and access. Consequently, all outdoor living area is oriented to the other side and rear of the home, making the usable yard area more private, livable, efficient, and appealing. Homes must be designed to take advantage of the side and rear orientations, usually by incorporating expanses of glass and easy access to the outdoors.

Home Type	Street	Approximate Net Density (Homes per acre)	Topography	Special Considerations
Single-family detached	Public or private, but public streets predominate	4.5 to 5.5	Flat topography with 0 percent to 5 percent slope is preferred	Requires carefully integrated architectural design, fence and wall design, and grading; landscaping is essential

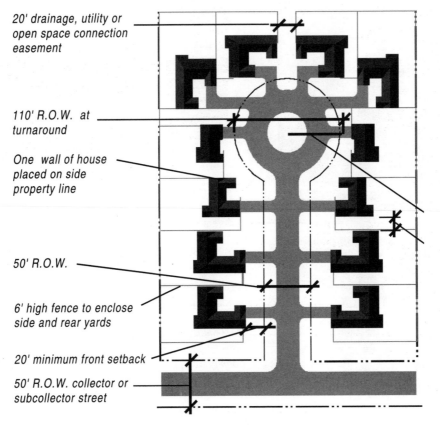

20' drainage, utility or open space connection easement

110' R.O.W. at turnaround

One wall of house placed on side property line

50' R.O.W.

6' high fence to enclose side and rear yards

20' minimum front setback

50' R.O.W. collector or subcollector street

45' radius to outside of turnaround pavement with center island

15' sideyard

Plan   Scale: 1" = 100'

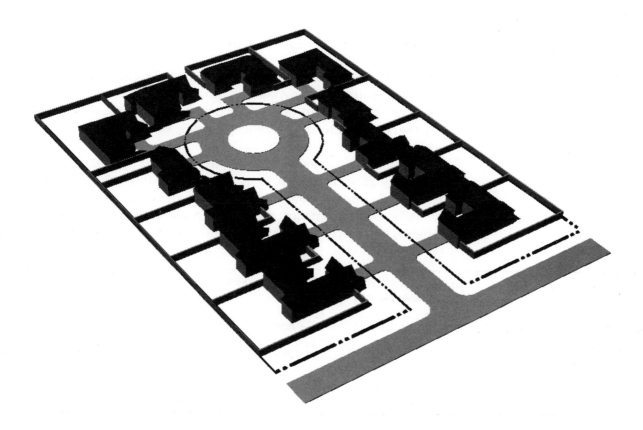

Home designed to take full advantage of the side and rear orientation

This design pattern allows for extensive treatment of outdoor living spaces and use areas with special paving, decks, trellises, pools, spas, and landscaping.

10. Detached "Z" Lot Homes

One variation of the zero lot-line home is the "Z" lot home, which has windows on all four sides while still providing complete privacy. The Z lot configuration also helps overcome one of the main problems with the original zero lot-line concept: a long, windowless wall on one side of the house.

The Z lot house is designed to be sited along the lot's diagonal axis so that the structure appears larger. Large expanses of glass admit natural light and integrate interior and exterior living spaces. As homesites become smaller, exterior open spaces should be carefully designed to include fences, decks, patios, and landscaping.

Home Type	Street	Approximate Net Density (Homes per acre)	Topography	Special Considerations
Single-family detached	Public	4.5 to 6.5	Flat topography with 0 percent to 5 percent slope is preferred	Requires carefully integrated architectural design, fence and wall design, and grading; landscaping is essential

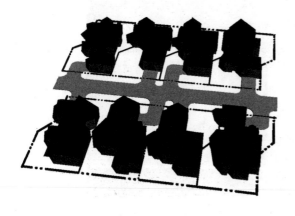

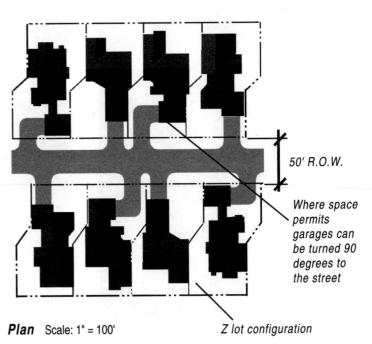

50' R.O.W.

Where space permits garages can be turned 90 degrees to the street

Z lot configuration

Plan   Scale: 1" = 100'

11. Detached Wide-Shallow Lot Homes

An alternative to the small-narrow lot layout is the wide-shallow lot, which resembles a Z lot turned parallel to the street. Homes sited on wide-shallow lots take advantage of their prominent front elevations and thus are not deep. While the houses convey an image reminiscent of the traditional single-family neighborhood, the shallow lots can mean increased densities and thereby reduce land costs. Yet, the densities and cost savings associated with wide-shallow lots are not as great as those associated with narrower homesites because of the additional road frontage required to serve each lot. When viewed from the street, however, wide-shallow lots are usually more appealing than narrower lots. The design of the homes, particularly the rear elevations, must be coordinated so that the rear windows of neighboring houses are not in direct alignment with one another; bedrooms are usually oriented to the front. Because outdoor living spaces are small, privacy fences are usually incorporated into the design.

Home Type	Street	Approximate Net Density (Homes per acre)	Topography	Special Considerations
Single-family detached	Public	4.5 to 6.0	Flat or rolling land is preferred	Requires carefully integrated architectural design, fence and wall design, and grading; landscaping is essential

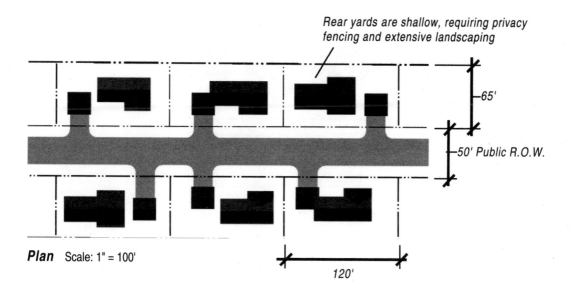

Rear yards are shallow, requiring privacy fencing and extensive landscaping

65'

50' Public R.O.W.

120'

Plan Scale: 1" = 100'

12. Detached Angled Z Lot Homes

Another variation of the zero lot-line house is the angled Z lot home, which is a modified Z lot home placed at an angle to the street. The house appears considerably wider because the front and side elevations are both visible at the same time. Angling the home creates landscaping pockets that help reduce the visual impact of the closely spaced homes. The angles also provide opportunities for exterior vistas and often take advantage of such amenities as waterfront views or golf courses.

Home Type	Street	Approximate Net Density (Homes per acre)	Topography	Special Considerations
Single-family detached	Public	4.5 to 6.5	Flat topography with a 0 percent to 5 percent slope is preferred	Requires carefully integrated architectural design, fence and wall design, and grading; landscaping is essential

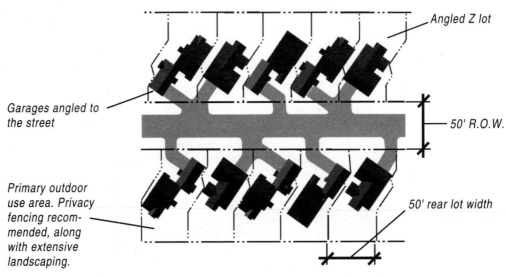

Angled Z lot

Garages angled to the street

50' R.O.W.

Primary outdoor use area. Privacy fencing recommended, along with extensive landscaping.

50' rear lot width

Plan   Scale: 1" = 100'

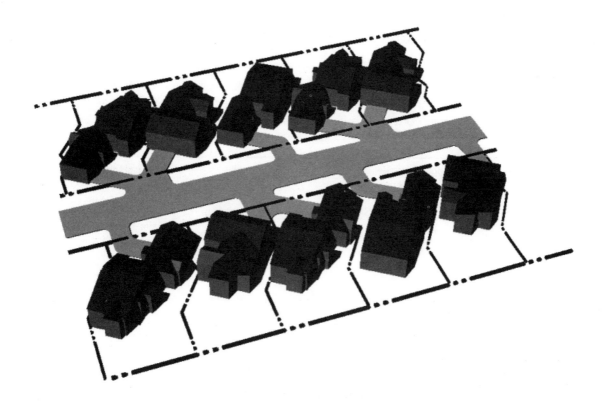

Angled Z lot also is adaptable to townhouse configuration.

Single-Family Attached Homes

13. Attached "Eyebrow" Homes

The eyebrow street configuration lends itself to a two- or three-unit attached home product often called a "duplex" or "triplex." Through careful architectural design and proper massing, these attached homes can convey a large-scale, single-family detached image.

Home Type	Street	Approximate Net Density (Homes per acre)	Topography	Special Considerations
Single-family attached	Private	4.5 to 6.0	Flat or rolling land is preferred	Requires careful architectural and site design; selective landscaping and fencing are essential

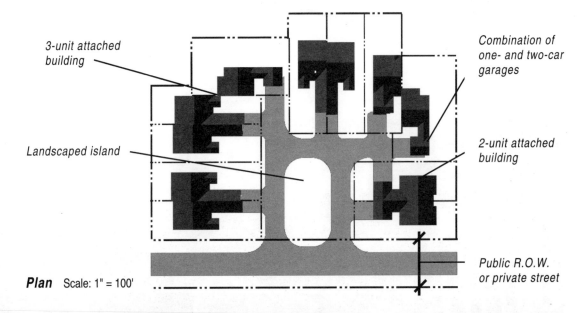

3-unit attached building

Landscaped island

Combination of one- and two-car garages

2-unit attached building

Public R.O.W. or private street

Plan   Scale: 1" = 100'

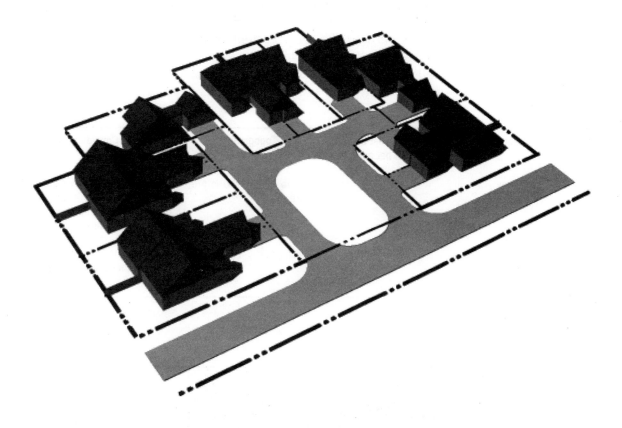

This cluster pattern is the building block of Summerlake retirement community in Fredericksburg, Virginia.

Developer: *The Silver Companies*
Architect: *Kaufman and Meeks*
Land Planners: *LDR International, Inc.*

14. Attached Homes With Private Parking Courts

This is perhaps the most cost-effective configuration for attached single-family homes or townhouses. This layout works particularly well as long as townhouse groups are kept to no more than six to eight units in a row.

Home Type	Street	Approximate Net Density (Homes per acre)	Topography	Special Considerations
Single-family attached (townhouse)	Private	10.0 to 12.0	Flat to rolling land is preferred	Lends itself to two-story townhouses with in-ground basements, two-and-one-half-story townhouses with in-ground basements, or two-story townhouses with walk-out basements as grade permits

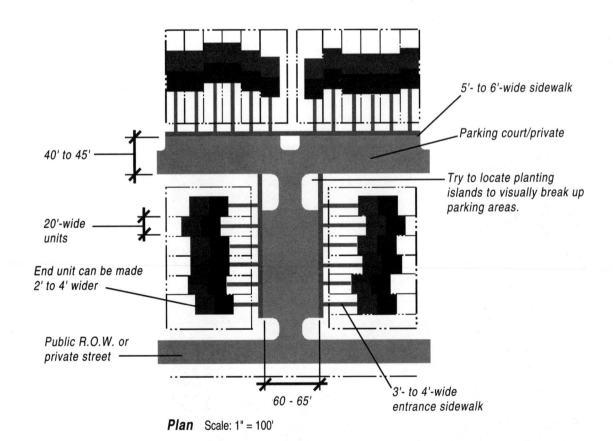

Plan   Scale: 1" = 100'

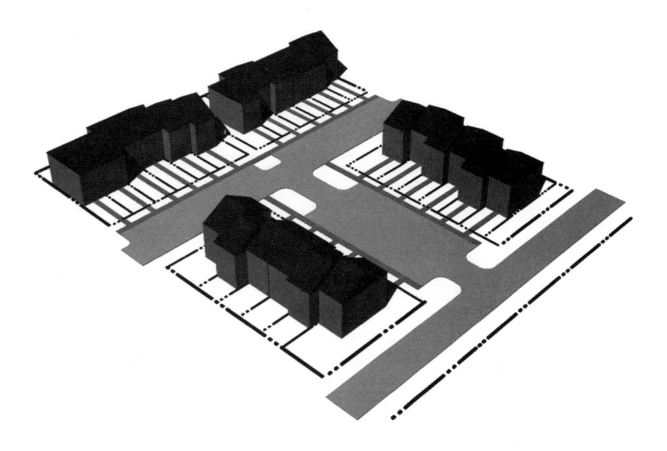

The overall site layout can be made more interesting by varying the pattern of each courtyard.

- Adapt the layout to the natural site features
- Add carports
- Landscaping, hedges, fences and walls should be integrated into the design

15. Attached Homes With Turnaround Streets

A variation of the private courtyard scheme, this pattern conveys more of a single-family image and works best when garages or carports are combined with surface parking. Some garages can be turned to create side-loaded, two-car garages.

Home Type	Street	Approximate Net Density (Homes per acre)	Topography	Special Considerations
Single-family attached (townhouse)	Public	7.0 to 9.0	Flat to rolling land is preferred, but steeply sloping land is acceptable if space is left between clusters to allow for gradient changes	Generally lends to itself more upscale townhouses

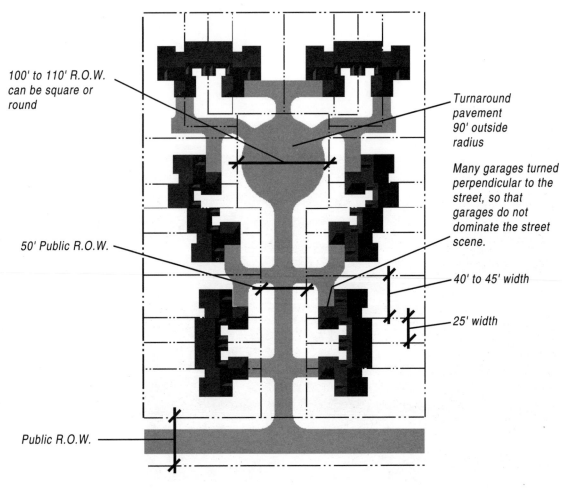

100' to 110' R.O.W. can be square or round

Turnaround pavement 90' outside radius

Many garages turned perpendicular to the street, so that garages do not dominate the street scene.

50' Public R.O.W.

40' to 45' width

25' width

Public R.O.W.

Plan   Scale: 1" = 100'

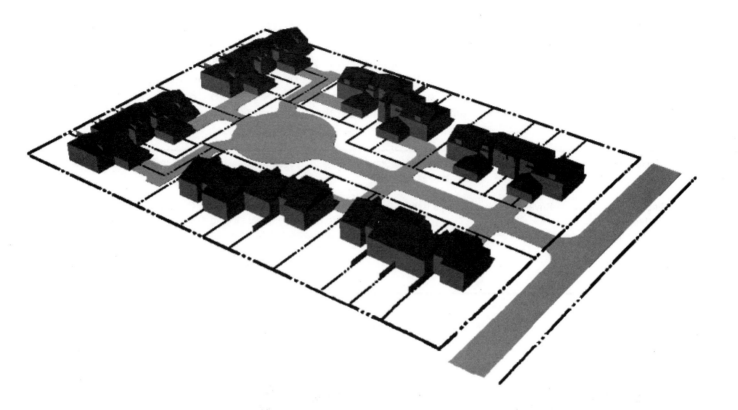

Too many garages on the public street dominate the street scene and restrict views of and pedestrian access to the homes.

16. Attached Homes With Automobile Courtyard

This pattern conveys a single-family image but at a slightly higher density than that permitted by the public street configuration. While well suited to the development of 25- to 28-foot-wide townhouses with integral garages, this pattern can also accommodate carports.

Home Type	Street	Approximate Net Density (Homes per acre)	Topography	Special Considerations
Single-family attached (townhouse)	Private	8.0 to 10.0	Flat to rolling land is preferred, but steeply sloping land is acceptable if space is left between clusters to allow for gradient changes	Generally lends to itself more upscale townhouses

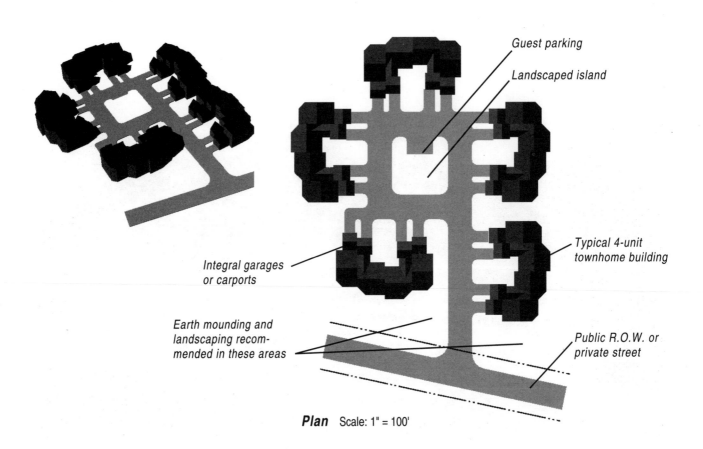

Guest parking

Landscaped island

Typical 4-unit townhome building

Integral garages or carports

Earth mounding and landscaping recommended in these areas

Public R.O.W. or private street

Plan   Scale: 1" = 100'

17. Attached Homes With Park Circle

A variation of the private courtyard scheme, this pattern illustrates how a larger turnaround circle can create a small park or open space area and become the focal point of a cluster. This pattern conveys a more urban feeling and is better sited on flatter land.

Home Type	Street	Approximate Net Density (Homes per acre)	Topography	Special Considerations
Single-family attached (townhouse)	Private or public	9.0 to 10.0	Flat to gently rolling land is preferred	Fences and landscaping are critical

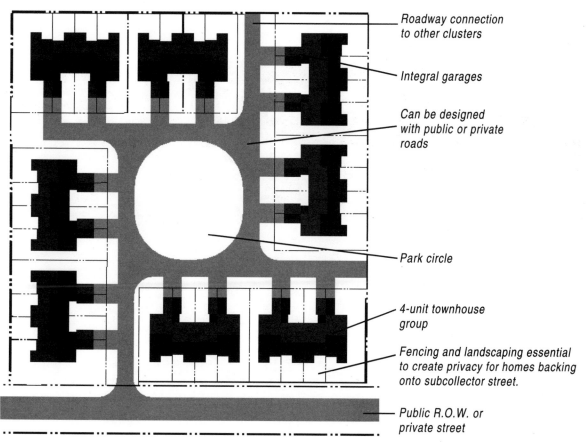

Roadway connection to other clusters

Integral garages

Can be designed with public or private roads

Park circle

4-unit townhouse group

Fencing and landscaping essential to create privacy for homes backing onto subcollector street.

Public R.O.W. or private street

Plan Scale: 1" = 100'

18. Attached Homes With Pedestrian Courtyard

This pattern creates a slightly higher density townhouse development. With its tightly clustered townhouses, the pedestrian courtyard creates a more interesting and highly detailed pedestrian space. One drawback, however, is that the layout concentrates parking in larger parking lots, which are sometimes difficult to make visually appealing.

Home Type	Street	Approximate Net Density (Homes per acre)	Topography	Special Considerations
Single-family attached (townhouse)	Private	14.0 to 15.0	Flat to rolling land is preferred	Parking areas must be designed with islands and landscaping; adaptable to affordable housing products

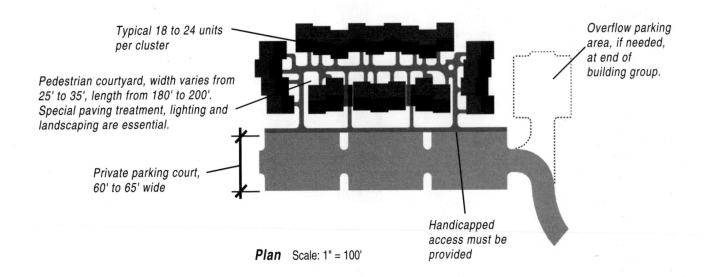

Typical 18 to 24 units per cluster

Pedestrian courtyard, width varies from 25' to 35', length from 180' to 200'. Special paving treatment, lighting and landscaping are essential.

Private parking court, 60' to 65' wide

Overflow parking area, if needed, at end of building group.

Handicapped access must be provided

Plan   Scale: 1" = 100'

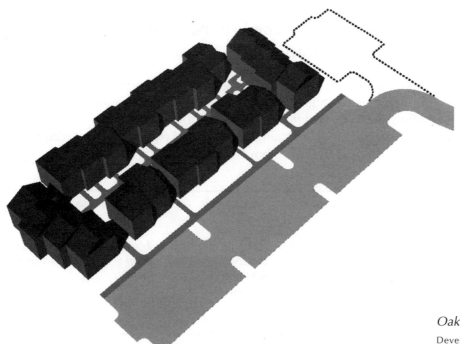

Oakwood, Fairfax County, Virginia.

Developer: *Porten Sullivan Corporation*
Architect: *CHK Architects*
Land Planners: *LDR International, Inc.*

19. "Turned" Attached Homes with Private Parking Court

A variation of the straight rectangular townhouse scheme is achieved by adding some angled units to the cluster group. The angled townhouse offers some interesting opportunities for site planning. The "turned" attached home, with its angled walls and expanded rear facade, also offers opportunities for innovative and exciting floor plans.

Home Type	Street	Approximate Net Density (Homes per acre)	Topography	Special Considerations
Single-family attached (townhouse)	Private	10.0 to 12.0	Flat, rolling, or steep land is acceptable with space between clusters	Adapts well to irregular topography or to irregularly shaped property

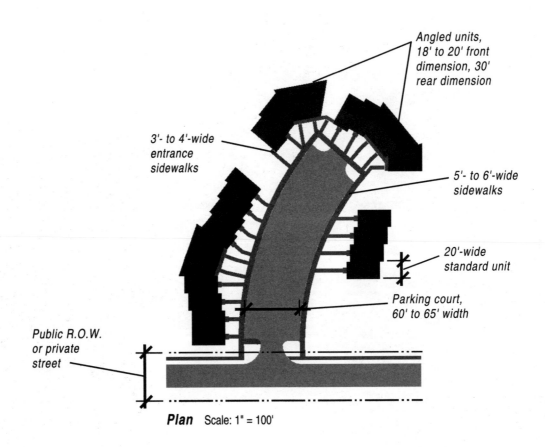

Angled units, 18' to 20' front dimension, 30' rear dimension

3'- to 4'-wide entrance sidewalks

5'- to 6'-wide sidewalks

20'-wide standard unit

Parking court, 60' to 65' width

Public R.O.W. or private street

Plan   Scale: 1" = 100'

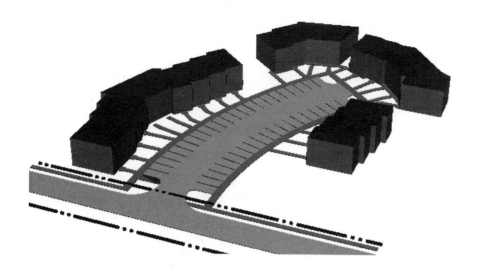

Front Elevation

Rear Elevation

Multifamily Stacked and Attached Homes

20. Stacked Quadrangle Homes

This quadrangle configuration adapts well to either flat topography or steeply sloping sites. It permits higher density without mass grading or the disturbance of natural land forms, even on steeply sloping land. This layout pattern is particularly attractive to homeowners whose active lifestyles demand limited home maintenance.

Home Type	Street	Approximate Net Density (Homes per acre)	Topography	Special Considerations
Multifamily attached and stacked	Private	14.0 to 16.0	Flat, rolling, or steep land	Requires sophisticated architectural design, grading, and site detailing

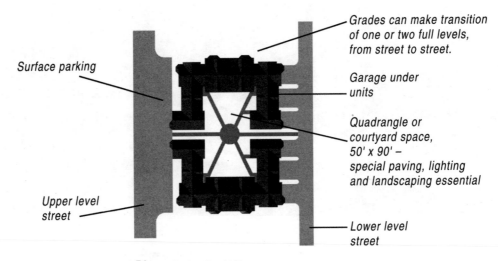

Surface parking

Upper level street

Grades can make transition of one or two full levels, from street to street.

Garage under units

Quadrangle or courtyard space, 50' x 90' – special paving, lighting and landscaping essential

Lower level street

Plan   Scale: 1" = 100'

Section   No Scale

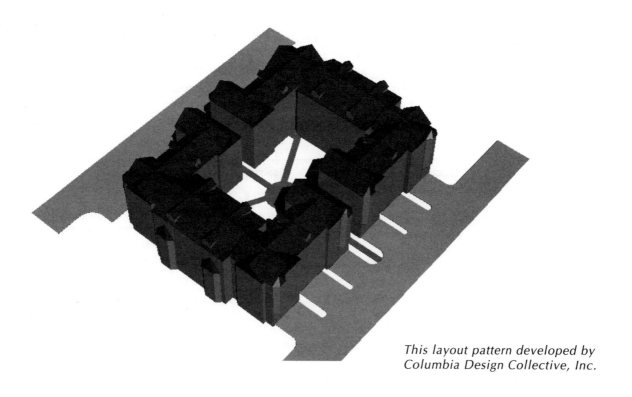

This layout pattern developed by Columbia Design Collective, Inc.

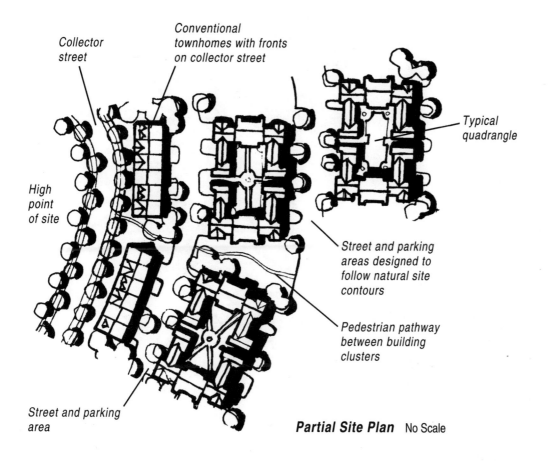

Collector street

Conventional townhomes with fronts on collector street

Typical quadrangle

High point of site

Street and parking areas designed to follow natural site contours

Pedestrian pathway between building clusters

Street and parking area

Partial Site Plan No Scale

21. Stacked and Attached Homes With Parking Courts

Some interesting architectural and site planning techniques are used today in multifamily housing to increase density while creating a more attractive look. The main site planning and architectural objective is to break up the massiveness of the buildings.

Home Type	Street	Approximate Net Density (Homes per acre)	Topography	Special Considerations
Stacked flats (apartments and condominiums)	Private	15.0 to 18.0	Flat to gently rolling land is preferred	Careful architectural design, site planning, and site detailing are necessary; landscaping is also essential

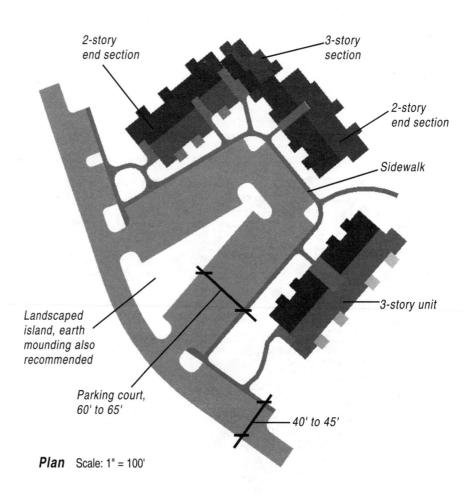

Plan   Scale: 1" = 100'

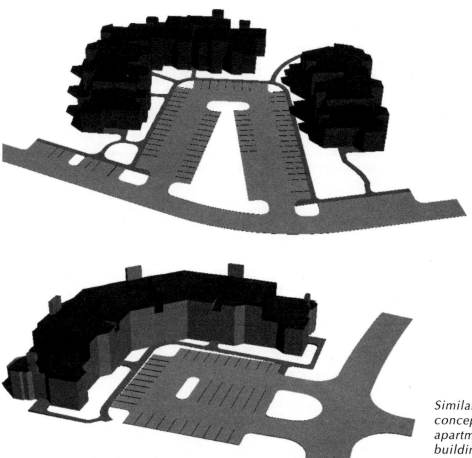

Similar to the "turned" townhome concept, angled stacked flats and apartment units can be used in a building group to create the "turned" building effect.

Chesapeake Harbour, Anne Arundel County, Maryland.

Developer: *Jerome J. Parks Companies*
Architect: *CHK Architects*
Land Planners: *LDR International, Inc.*

Mixed Residential Types

22. Single-Family Attached and Multifamily Stacked Homes With Park Square

This unique density scheme accommodates a mix of residential designs. It is most applicable to fairly flat land and is adaptable to infill projects, particularly in urban areas.

Home Type	Street	Approximate Net Density (Homes per acre)	Topography	Special Considerations
Mix of attached single-family homes and stacked flats	Combination of public and private	12.0 to 16.0	Flat to gently rolling land is preferred	Requires careful integration of architectural design and site planning; site detailing and landscaping are critical

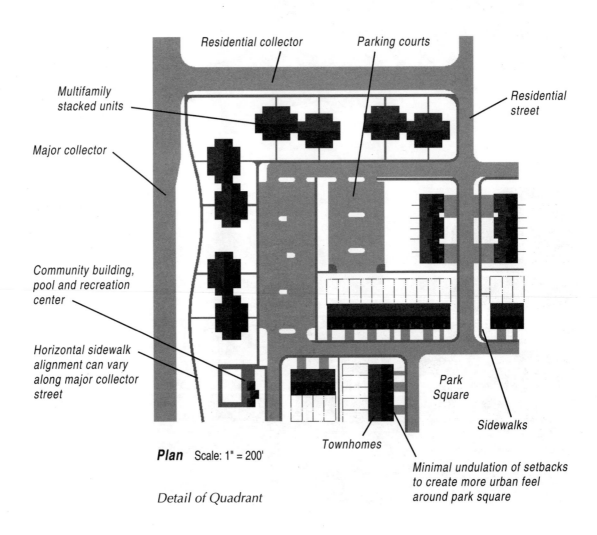

Residential collector

Parking courts

Multifamily stacked units

Residential street

Major collector

Community building, pool and recreation center

Horizontal sidewalk alignment can vary along major collector street

Park Square

Sidewalks

Townhomes

Minimal undulation of setbacks to create more urban feel around park square

Plan   Scale: 1" = 200'

Detail of Quadrant

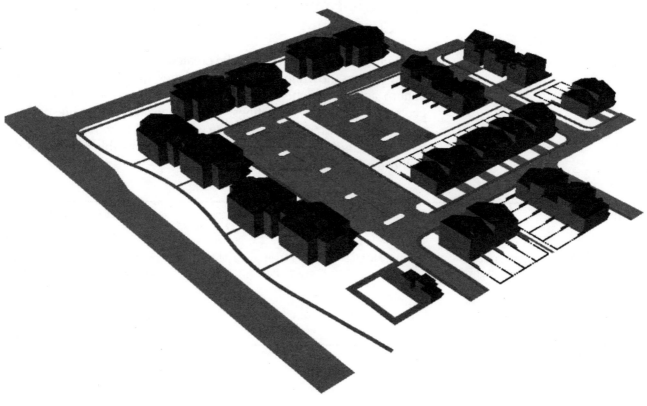

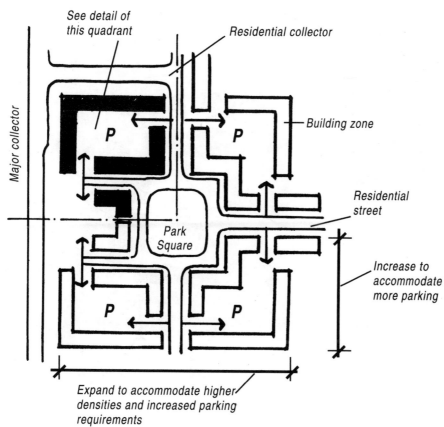

See detail of this quadrant

Residential collector

Major collector

Building zone

P

P

Residential street

Park Square

P

P

Increase to accommodate more parking

Expand to accommodate higher densities and increased parking requirements

23. Single-Family Attached Homes With Mid-Rise Cluster

An interesting configuration can be created by mixing attached single-family homes (townhouses) with a higher mid-rise building. This pattern achieves higher density solutions close to activity or retail centers in more urban settings. It offers an alternative lifestyle for today's active homeowners or those who prefer limited home maintenance. The mid-rise component is especially adaptable for the elderly or those who require assisted living.

Home Type	Street	Approximate Net Density (Homes per acre)	Topography	Special Considerations
Mix of attached single-family homes and stacked flats (mid-rise)	Combination of public and private	15.0 to 20.0	Flat to gently rolling land is preferred	Requires careful integration of architectural design and site planning; site detailing and landscaping are critical

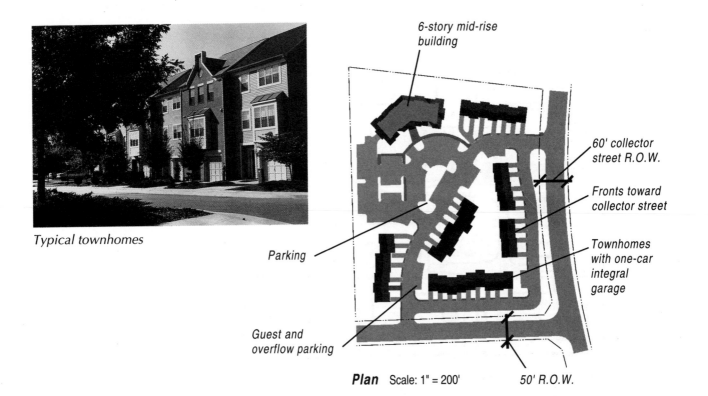

Typical townhomes

6-story mid-rise building

60' collector street R.O.W.

Fronts toward collector street

Townhomes with one-car integral garage

Parking

Guest and overflow parking

Plan   Scale: 1" = 200'

50' R.O.W.

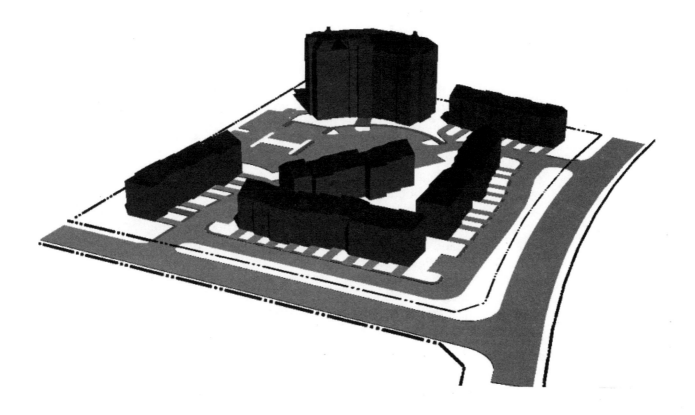

Kingsgate, Columbia, Maryland

Developer: *BBI Homes*
Architect: *Columbia Design Collective*

24. Single-Family Detached and Attached Homes in Traditional Neighborhood Block

This pattern, prevalent in most American cities, has emerged as a scheme that offers small-town charm. It allows a fuller integration of residential product types and creates a sense of neighborhood. One word of caution is, however, in order. Recent experience with this type of layout, which is organized around gridded streets and alleys, indicates that infrastructure costs generally may run higher than for a street or cul-de-sac cluster scheme. The cost differential is due primarily to the excessive street standards required by most suburban jurisdictions. To justify increased site development costs, townhouses and higher density detached homes are most compatible with this configuration.

Home Type	Street	Approximate Net Density (Homes per acre)	Topography	Special Considerations
Single-family detached and attached	Public or public-private combination	5.0 to 10.0	Flat land is preferred	Requires careful integration of architectural design and site planning; demands more reasonable street standards; can accommodate accessory units

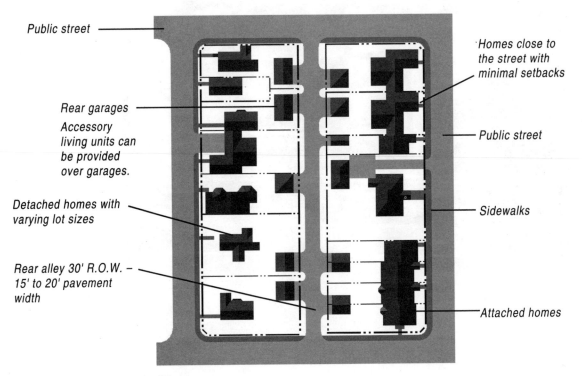

Public street

Homes close to the street with minimal setbacks

Rear garages

Accessory living units can be provided over garages.

Public street

Detached homes with varying lot sizes

Sidewalks

Rear alley 30' R.O.W. – 15' to 20' pavement width

Attached homes

Plan   Scale: 1" = 100'

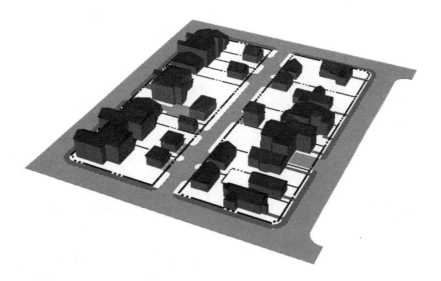

This pattern is one of the building blocks for the Kentlands in Gaithersburg, Maryland.

Architects : *Andres Duany and Elizabeth Plater-Zyberk*
Developer: *Joseph Alfandre & Company, Inc.*

Typical street-side view

Typical view of a rear alley

25. Traditional Neighborhood Cluster Street

A variation of the conventional neighborhood block, the street and alley scheme is the traditional neighborhood cluster pattern. It creates the charm and scale of the small town while reducing the requirements for infrastructure development. This particular pattern is more adaptable to rolling topography than to the straight grid system and is well suited to infill development.

Home Type	Street	Approximate Net Density (Homes per acre)	Topography	Special Considerations
Single-family detached and attached	Public	4.0 to 6.0	Flat land is preferred	Requires careful integration of architectural design and site planning; demands more reasonable street standards; can accommodate accessory units

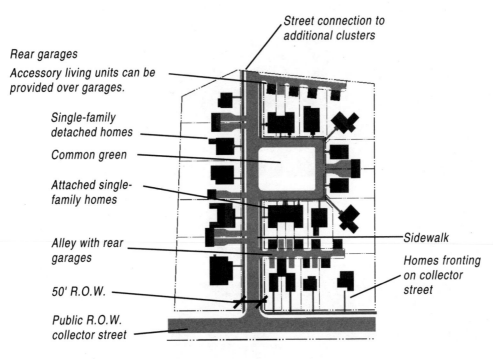

Street connection to additional clusters

Rear garages

Accessory living units can be provided over garages.

Single-family detached homes

Common green

Attached single-family homes

Alley with rear garages

50' R.O.W.

Public R.O.W. collector street

Sidewalk

Homes fronting on collector street

Plan Scale: 1" = 200'

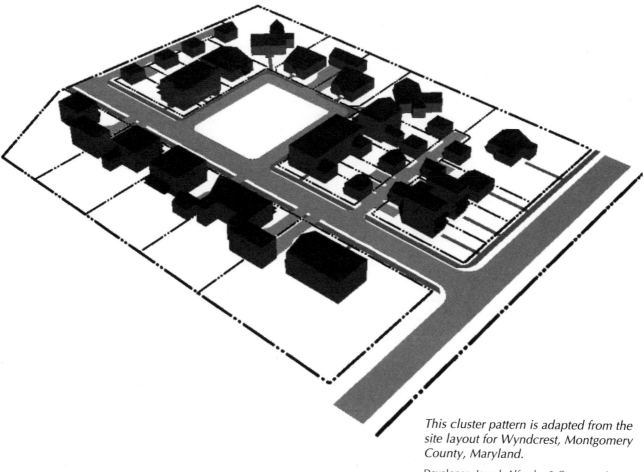

This cluster pattern is adapted from the site layout for Wyndcrest, Montgomery County, Maryland.

Developer: *Joseph Alfandre & Company, Inc.*

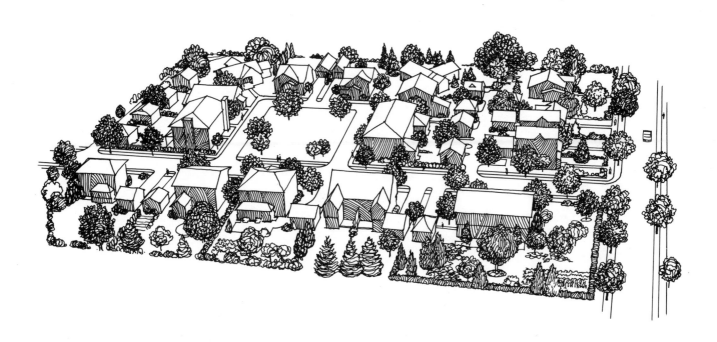

Community Planning for the Future

In this chapter:

- Reversing Excess Land Consumption
- Inner City Housing and Edge Cities
- More Compact Development
- Adequate Public Facilities
- Statewide Growth Management Programs
- Environmental Balance
- The Need for New Planning Models
- Creating Vision and Value

The home building industry is subject to constant change as market conditions fluctuate and new patterns of household formation evolve. The 1990 U.S. Census provides evidence that the housing market is changing: average household size is smaller; the percent of working mothers is increasing; and the percent of "traditional" households (two adults with children) is decreasing. The census also reveals that housing costs are continuing to outpace income growth; that more commuters are traveling in single-occupant vehicles; and that the number of vehicles per household is increasing.

Forward-looking communities are working to shape future residential development in an effort to improve the quality of their citizens' lives. Based on both the lessons learned from our most livable communities and a growing consensus that our environment is worth protecting, future goals for community planning are likely to include the following:

- The communities of the future should be more compact and less land-consuming.

- Existing infrastructure, which represents past public investment, should be used efficiently; new infrastructure investment should be planned carefully.

- While recognizing that any development necessarily involves some level of disturbance of the land and use of resources, well-designed communities of the future should be more compatible with the environment as well as more energy efficient.

- Strategies for reducing automobile dependence should be incorporated into land plans wherever possible, encouraging transit-related development and the planning of pedestrian-friendly, mixed-use communities.

TILLY by Berry & Holub

Printed by permission of Hugh Holub.

Reversing Excess Land Consumption

Now more than ever, Americans are planning, lobbying, and zoning for controlled growth. Nonetheless, each of us is using nearly twice the amount of land as we did 40 years ago – and some studies suggest that each new resident averages nearly four times as much land consumption because of the sprawling pattern of new development. A Maryland study of the Chesapeake Bay watershed found that, in 1950, each resident of new development consumed 0.18 acres of land; in 1990, the average was 0.65 acres (see Figure 7.1).

Unlike physical pollutants such as nutrients in sewage, poorly planned land development patterns cannot be reversed simply by eliminating the source. Property rights and multiple ownership patterns make existing land use patterns difficult to change. Today's land use decisions will have consequences for many decades: more paved surfaces, high energy demand, increased pollution from automobiles, more sediment in waterways, and escalating public service costs. Most important, sprawl development represents underuse of a valuable and finite resource – land.

Reduced per-person land consumption is one of the essential ingredients in creating more livable, environmentally sound, and economically viable communities. By changing our patterns of land use we may also be able to alleviate – at least partially – other excesses such as automobile dependence and energy consumption.

Inner City Housing and Edge Cities

As the financial and environmental cost of developing raw land increases, reclaiming already-developed land will become a more feasible and attractive housing option. Already, many communities are considering plans to convert abandoned industrial areas and other vacant or underused downtown land for residential use. Amenities, convenience to employment centers, and proximity to services are key considerations in planning in-town housing.

In the areas emerging at the periphery of the nation's older urban cores, residential development is an essential element. In his book *Edge City,* Joel Garreau defines the edge city as a concentrated node with at least 5 million square feet of office space, 600,000 square feet of retail space, and higher density residential development. In many of today's edge cities, the residential areas are characterized by compact, high-quality development. This trend is likely to continue as edge cities evolve and become more competitive. The challenge is to make these intense mixed-use concentrations attractive to residents, workers, and shoppers. In these communities, a goal of future development is to provide people-friendly buildings, image-making focal points, and gathering places that enhance the appeal of these edge cities for residents, employees, and visitors alike.

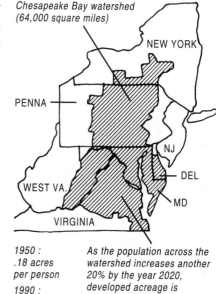

Chesapeake Bay watershed (64,000 square miles)

NEW YORK

PENNA

NJ

DEL

MD

WEST VA.

VIRGINIA

1950 :
.18 acres
per person

1990 :
.65 acres
per person

As the population across the watershed increases another 20% by the year 2020, developed acreage is projected to increase by 60%

Figure 7.1
Consumption of Land within the Chesapeake Bay Watershed

Source: *Turning The Tide,* Saving the Chesapeake Bay, data according to the "2020 REPORT" on population growth issued in 1989 by the State of Maryland.

More Compact Development

For many years, planners have advocated more compact residential development patterns. Particularly when linked to improved public transit, higher densities can relieve traffic congestion, provide affordable housing opportunities, reduce land consumption, and require less infrastructure. But, until recently, high-density neighborhoods have been viewed as less desirable, less "livable" places.

Now a convergence of their varied interests has formed an alliance among planners, builders seeking ways to deal with the high costs of development and the problems of environmental regulation, conservationists seeking to curb sprawl, and public officials seeking solutions to fiscal problems. The challenge facing this alliance is to create communities that are truly livable, to achieve densities higher than those permitted in the standard suburb, and to find workable solutions to such problems as traffic congestion and the lack of affordable housing.

The neotraditional towns, pedestrian pockets, and rural villages described in chapter 2 represent efforts to create new models; the success of these new models will be evaluated as new prototype developments are completed. In the years ahead, we can expect to see other innovations in large-scale community planning that achieve more compactness while preserving the qualities considered essential for livability. At the same time, individual builders will continue to improve upon designs for housing types such as small-lot houses, townhouses, garden apartments, and condominiums. Greater mixing of housing types will become more commonplace. Enthusiastic buyer response, particularly to innovations that address environmental concerns, will inspire further exploration and improvement.

Adequate Public Facilities

Nearly every large and small town, city, and county today is managing growth in one form or another. The most common goals of such management activity are adequate infrastructure and maintenance or improvement of neighborhood quality. Planned unit developments, cluster zoning, and adequate facility requirements are methods commonly used to further these goals.

Adequate facility requirements may be general statements of goals in the comprehensive plans or zoning and subdivision regulations. They sometimes are elaborated into highly specific goals, policies, and standards in the comprehensive plans or specialized adequate public facility ordinances (APFOs). Adequate facility requirements may be stand-alone systems directed at controlling offsite impacts on a case-by-case basis. They also may be part of an integrated growth management program that includes growth phasing limits or stated growth rates. The great variability in the content and application of adequate facility requirements makes it imperative that each local jurisdiction formulate its own policies to address the specific situation.

Statewide Growth Management Programs

Even with the evolution of environmental regulations, regional planning, and local growth management over the past two decades, some states have found that further planning controls are warranted. As of 1992, the following states have enacted statewide growth management programs: Oregon, Florida, New Jersey, Maine, Vermont, Rhode Island, Georgia, Washington State and Hawaii (see Figure 7.2). Other states with some form of comprehensive growth legislation include California, Maryland, Massachusetts, and New York. These programs are designed to advance comprehensive land use planning and fill in the gaps between state environmental regulation, regional planning, and scattered local growth management efforts.

A comparison of state-sponsored growth management systems reveals a wide diversity in program features and provisions. The states that have adopted such programs and legislation vary widely in population, growth rates, and density. Almost all growth-management states, however, have important natural resources. For example, almost all of these states have substantial seacoast or lakeside regions, environmental attributes that are closely linked to the states' economies through recreation and tourism. Other states with significant environmental resources and tourism economies are likely candidates for future state-sponsored growth management programs. Such states include Colorado, New Hampshire, Virginia, Michigan, and North Carolina.

In the near future, however, the trend is away from state-dominant models and toward models emphasizing local cooperation and negotiation. Whether local or state-sponsored, growth-management regulations will have an affect on housing availability and affordability, growth patterns, infrastructure investment, and fiscal stability.

Figure 7.2   States with Statewide Growth Management Programs or Comprehensive Growth Legislation
Source: LDR International, Inc.

Environmental Balance

In the years ahead, the home building industry will continue to be heavily affected by environmental regulations. The challenge in formulating and implementing regulations is to achieve an appropriate balance between protecting the environment and accommodating human needs and desires. Further, future policy decisions about the environment may lead to changes in some of the commonly accepted standards for local development ordinances, clearing the way for more creative approaches to community planning.

The following discussion highlights areas of environmental concern that can be expected to influence community planning and development methods significantly in the coming years.

Wetlands. Governments at all levels have enacted wetlands regulations aimed at avoiding or minimizing environmental impacts. Under the Clean Water Act, the federal government regulates any filling activity within wetlands. States that have promulgated nontidal wetlands regulations typically expand the types of activities that require state permits. Many local jurisdictions also require wetlands buffers and setbacks. The proliferation of wetlands regulations has created one of the most difficult approval processes the development community has ever faced. In almost every instance, developers and builders are required to mitigate any wetlands disturbance. Additions and changes to the regulatory procedures can be expected.

Forest conservation. In response to concerns about global warming, compromised air quality, habitat destruction, and increased soil erosion and sedimentation, tree preservation has become a growing issue throughout the United States. Several local jurisdictions have already enacted tree preservation ordinances. In 1991, Maryland passed the nation's first statewide forest conservation and reforestation bill; other states are likely to follow.

The building community must be prepared to deal with the economic burden and increased approval time created by forest conservation legislation. At the same time, the building industry should consider the positive impacts associated with forest conservation measures. Trees planted or retained on newly developed sites can increase real estate values, offer curb appeal, and enhance home energy efficiency. The clustering techniques explained in this book can be used to respond to forest preservation requirements.

Water conservation. Population increases coupled with limited groundwater and surface water supplies have led to water crises in many areas of the United States. Several states, including Florida, are now drafting water-use standards. Southern California's Water-Efficient Landscape Ordinance will regulate the design, installation, and maintenance of landscaping in new projects and provide guidelines for water management practices and waste prevention for established landscapes. In the future, water conservation legislation is likely to mandate land planning and site design practices that conserve water.

Air quality. The 1990 revision of the federal Clean Air Act strengthened many of the original act's provisions and added new ones. Of particular concern to the home building industry are the pollution control requirements for cities that have not attained federal air quality standards. Regulations designed to place more stringent controls on automobile emissions may include development provisions limiting uses that generate automotive traffic. In the future, stricter enforcement can be expected, and developers will likely be required to demonstrate that new development will help maintain or reduce automobile emission levels.

Critical environmental areas. A critical environmental area (CEA) designation is a tool for regulating environmentally sensitive portions of land. Florida's 1972 Environmental Land and Water Management Act and Maryland's 1984 Chesapeake Bay Critical Area Protection Law provide for CEA designation of clearly specified areas. In the future, more states are likely to enact similar legislation. Though generally opposed by the building industry, CEA regulations ideally provide a comprehensive view of all the environmental factors affecting development in a specific area and thus can allow for more informed decisions that encourage rational development and accelerate the permitting process.

Rural Open Space Preservation. In many urbanizing areas of the country, communities are struggling to balance the need for residential and commercial development against the desire for preservation of agricultural lands, scenic open spaces, and other unique land resources. Several jurisdictions have adopted a variety of techniques to promote open space preservation. Techniques include easements, large-lot zoning, rural village ordinances, transfer of development rights (TDRs), and growth management plans.

The home building industry can expect that various preservation organizations and special interest groups will continue to undertake efforts to preserve open space. The problem is not growth itself but the pattern of growth – uniform and unbroken large-lot development – that has occurred under conventional zoning practices. Conservationists who realize that stopping growth is an unachievable objective can be expected to work with developers and builders to advocate sensible growth solutions and to educate government officials and the public about such solutions.

The Need for New Planning Models

In the years ahead, more communities will seek models for community planning that create coalitions of diverse interests and build consensus around a shared vision of the community's future. Builders and local officials, planners, environmentalists, and citizens' groups are beginning to recognize the advantages of working together to devise new patterns of residential and community development that satisfy all interests. Experience suggests that all interests must remain sensitive to:

- *Rapid changes.* In the normal course of a three- to four-year comprehensive planning process, rapidly changing factors can make a plan obsolete the day it is approved.

- *Increasing regional constraints.* Regulations that govern environmental preservation, wetlands protection, regional sanitation, and traffic will play a greater role in determining the range of acceptable land development activities.

- *Resistance to change.* Rather than engaging in visionary leadership, elected leaders and public agencies tend to focus on preserving the status quo as they struggle against fiscal constraints and day-to-day crises.

- *New players.* Institutions, investors, and landowners with large landholdings are becoming players in the development industry. Most of these new players lack real estate experience and must learn the development process.

- *More sophisticated developers.* Faced with mounting economic and regulatory pressures, most successful developers have grown to include in-house personnel and resources to undertake larger-scale planning.

Comprehensive planning is no longer the exclusive domain of the public sector; increasingly, the private sector will become involved in planning activities and may even assume a leadership role. The major challenge is how communities can fuse private sector interests with public goals.

Creating Vision and Value

A streamlined, systematic, and strategic community planning process applicable to urban, suburban, and rural settings will point the way to the future. This process can be successfully employed to plan and develop urban infill sites as well as to prepare comprehensive growth plans for entire counties. Following the seven steps listed on the next page should encourage active and continuous community participation.

1. Organize. Get ready by creating public-private coalitions and special planning advisory councils, defining the process, and designating team members.

2. Strategize. Conduct a preliminary strategic assessment to identify issues, establish goals and objectives, and fine tune the work program. Identify opportunities. Emphasize the importance of listening to citizens and community leaders.

3. Visualize. Develop quick alternatives and create a vision. Prepare three-dimensional images and use state-of-the-art presentation techniques to transmit the vision.

4. Commit. Sell the ideas, build consensus, identify leadership, and find ways to gain support--including financial support--throughout the process.

5. Refine. Test alternative concepts, refine the preferred development approach, and prepare promotional graphics, technical data, and documentation to convert the vision into sound plans and strategies.

6. Endorse. Gain widespread support for the plan and for the implementation strategies. Organize the formal approval processes leading to adoption and implementation.

7. Implement. Develop a complete and detailed implementation strategy and action plan (who does what, where, and when) to bring about successful implementation to achieve sustained momentum.

The Successful Site Planning and Community Design Process   Source: LDR International, Inc.

Additional Reading

Brandes, Donald and Luzier, J. Michael, *Developing Difficult Sites: Solutions for Developers and Builders,* NAHB, 1991.

Downs, Anthony, *The Need for a New Vision for the Development of Large U.S. Metropolitan Areas, Salomon Brothers,* 1989.

Duany, A., et. al. "Zoning for Traditional Neighborhoods," in *Land Development,* Fall 1992.

Gale, Dennis, "Eight State-Sponsored Growth Management Programs," in *Journal of the American Planning Association,* Autumn 1992.

Garreau, Joel, *Edge City,* Doubleday, 1991.

Higher Density Housing, NAHB, 1986.

Horton, Tom and Eichbaum, William, *Turning the Tide,* Chesapeake Bay Foundation, 1991.

Lewis, Ralph, *Land Buying Checklist,* NAHB, 1990.

Land Development, 7th edition, NAHB, 1987.

Residential Streets, American Society of Civil Engineers, NAHB & ULI, 2nd ed., 1990.

Yaro, Robert D., *Dealing with Change in the Connecticut River Valley: A Design Manual For Conservation and Development,* Center for Rural Massachusetts, 1988.

Affordable Residential Land Development: A Guide for local Government and Developers, NAHB National Research Center, 1987.